I0434706

Mid-East Meets West

Mid-East Meets West

◆

On Being and Becoming a Modern Arab American

Sally Bishai

iUniverse, Inc.

New York Lincoln Shanghai

Mid-East Meets West
On Being and Becoming a Modern Arab American

All Rights Reserved © 2004 by Sally Bishai

No part of this book may be reproduced or transmitted in any form or by any means, graphic, electronic, or mechanical, including photocopying, recording, taping, or by any information storage retrieval system, without the written permission of the publisher.

iUniverse, Inc.

For information address:
iUniverse, Inc.
2021 Pine Lake Road, Suite 100
Lincoln, NE 68512
www.iuniverse.com

ISBN: 0-595-31731-6 (pbk)
ISBN: 0-595-66400-8 (cloth)

Printed in the United States of America

For the **Rev. Samuel Wahby**, who touched so many lives during his own, mine included…I can't wait to see you again, Baba *habibi*…:)

Contents

Section One: Before We Jump to the Fun Stuff, We'll Have to Get Some Groundwork Out of the Way…

Section 2: Hurdles—You Have to Understand This Stuff Before You Can Get Anywhere.

Section 3: Roadblocks—The Issues Faced by Arab Americans

Acknowledgements

It's never easy to write one of these—not so much because you feel that no one's helped you, but because you feel that *everyone's* helped you:

- The friends (and family!) that stayed up nights with you by phone, holding the line while you jotted down that particularly terrific sentence—making sure you got it right and listening to it once, twice—and assuring you that it made sense and sounded great.

- Other friends who came up with catchy titles and angles that you hadn't thought of in the least (despite your alleged expertise in one topic or another).

- Still other friends that you only saw every so often, but whose very presence and conversations set chain reactions off in your brain, reminding you of thoughts you had at 3 a.m. a few months back, inspiring you when you thought you'd run out of ideas.

- The colleagues that you worked with and spoke to on a regular basis, who, unbeknownst to them, encouraged you with a word or expression.

- The supervisors and professors who became more like friends and mentors—verging on family, perhaps—without knowing it.

To this end, I would like to say **thank you** to all of the people who've touched my life during "The Pensacola Chapter," but especially:

God, who should obviously be first in everything, because without Him, we'd not be here to actually *do* anything, but esp*ecially* since He falls into each of the five above categories; also, because I'm so grateful to Him for everything, His presence most of all.

My **family**, (especially *The Children*) for loving me so much. For putting up with so much. For being so generous to me. For "sheltering" me in that patently 50's *Saiidi* Egyptian way, so much so that I got frustrated with life and wrote this book (*bahebokom bishakl!*); also for their love, support, friendship and existence in my life.

My beloved **Mama** and **Baba**, and every one of my dear uncles—**Victor, Mofied, Wafeek, and Hany**—for their love, support, knowledge and great ideas (*bahebokom kaman bishakl*—SSSSS).

"The Egyptians," every one of them, but especially **Eman, Ezzat, Mina and Ustina**, for their friendship, love, support, proofreading, suggestions, jokes and *mahshi*; **Soher (and her lovely family)**, for her friendship and support during my pilot study and the early stages of this book, for introducing me to so many people, and for treating me like family; **Maha** and **Youssef**, who dragged me into the pool (clothes and all!) and rescued me from 2,000 pages of research (*and* were dear friends, to boot); **Nermine, Hany** and **Nagy**, who inspired me to expound upon the Chaldeans and Copts; **Aboona Youstos**, who is the best Aboona in the world; and all of the rest of the **Egyptians** who filled my days with laughter and love (*yalla, bil marra—ba7ebokom into kaman!*).

My (heretofore unmentioned) dearest friends and/or favorite people—**Linda** (S.B.), **Dr. Cryer, Dr. Troy (U), Dr. Rovick, Svetlana, Akram, Carlos, Maged** (*ya kharabi!*), **Sam, Aaron, David, Mourad, Matthew, T-Bone,** and **the Bassetts** (and also **Ragheb Alama, Amr Diab** and **Mostafa Amar,** each of whom kept me company when I thought I'd never finish!)—each of whom cheered me on (at some point), listened to me carry on about deadlines and the like (before threatening me with duct tape, ha ha), and who made me want to finish. Lots of love to each of you!

Sam again, for giving me great ideas, a (very) different perspective, and a title!

My **students**, who "got to" hear so many examples from my own life that they could pen a sequel to this book.

Dr. Tammy Swenson Lepper, for being the first professor in my entire life to extract an academic paper from me—and also, for being on my committee, not to mention being helpful and kind in the process. *And* for being like a big sister to me.

Dr. Amir Karimi, whose friendship, advice and moral support have meant so much to me.

All of the people whose stories and opinions have been included in this book—may God bless you and keep you!

And finally the professors who went above and beyond the call of duty, offering support, advice, and friendship—in essence making this book possible—**Dr. Mohammed El-Nawawy** (who made my Master's possible) and **Dr. Bruce Swain** (the best person in the whole world, who made my Ph.D. possible)—both of whom I've declared family members, and whom I adore, *and* whom I suspect of being angels (they've certainly blessed my life!).

Again, many thanks and lots of love to everyone—*Rabinah yi barikkom*!

:)

SB, November 2003

Preface

My parents left Alexandria, Egypt in the mid-1970s and immigrated to America, land of opportunity. Mr. Stork dropped me off a few years later, and that was that.

I never gave a thought, growing up, to the fact that I spoke an extra language and spent my summers sniffing jasmine flowers and getting a tan on the Mediterranean while my classmates visited grandparents in Virginia and went on Carnival Cruises. It didn't really *occur* to me that my life was any different from the lives of my schoolmates, all of whom were American as apple pie, just as their great-grandparents and *their* great-grandparents had been. In fact, it didn't really occur to me until I noticed the opposite sex.

The ban on concerts, dating, slumber parties and going to the mall with the girls got me thinking a little, but nothing philosophical. More along the lines of "Oh, how I *hate* this! What did I *ever* do to deserve this oppression?!" than anything else.

Then I noticed how interested Americans were to hear about my "plight." "How do Egyptians get married?" they would wonder, fascinated. "You mean you're really not allowed to date?!" they would ask me, incredulous. And I, ever the raconteur, explained things. Then, around the time I started college, my mind wandered and I forgot about the whole "bicultural thing."

But a few years later, I started thinking seriously about biculturalism. I analyzed, deconstructed, and kicked around enough ideas to give me a headache. When it was all over, all I had was the headache.

So I figured I'd drop it (again) and move on to other things, like psychology, writing and photography. And I did.

Then, it was time for graduate school (and the inevitable move across the state). The first people I saw on the first day in my first apartment *ever* were Egyptians. One family, to be precise. One week later, my parents had finished moving me into my new home and who should knock on my door—but more Egyptians? One week later, yet *another* family moved into the same apartment complex—can you guess their nationality? I wasn't surprised when, a week after *that*, I was helping this newest family find work and we ran into a nice Pakistani man who directed us to *another* Egyptian family who had another Egyptian friend, who had a *sister* who came for visits.

Then, we discovered a church (this whole assembly was Coptic Orthodox, by the way) one hour away. In that place I found a few kindred spirits who invited me to yet another church yet *another* hour away. So, in the space of about three months, I found that I was surrounded by over 300 Egyptian Christians, apart from the hundred or so I'd previously gotten to hang out with during my travels around the States. This is to say nothing about the Syrians, Saudis and Jordanians I've also run into. And the Moroccans that keep appearing, and the Palestinians. And the Lebanese…

And so you see why I could not leave this topic alone. You see how patterns forced themselves upon me, beseeching me to notice them and commit them to paper. And by the time you finish this book, you'll see how biculturalism has affected *my* life (and maybe your own).

Interestingly enough, I never would have made the move and researched this topic *and* found my clan of Egyptians had I not met a very kind professor who took the time to talk some sense into me—and assuage my parents' fears about the field I wanted to enter, and more importantly, the move across the state.

Interestingly enough, *he* was from Alexandria, too.

Letter to The Reader

Ok, so not *all* of you fit into one category, whether in terms of nationality, upbringing, immigration status, or reason for reading, even.

After all, some of you will be non-Arabs of any bent, whether Western or not. Others of you will be "first generation Americans," that is, born in the United States to immigrant parents, or perhaps you're a second-or third-generation American. Some of you may have moved over here as kids or teenagers. Others of you may have come over in your thirties or forties. Subsequently, you may have oodles of experience with Arabs, or none at all.

In any case, I'd like to thank you for picking this book up. It's a reflection of the life experiences of hundreds of Americans whose roots lie half the world away. It also includes many of the pitfalls that Arab Americans are prone to stumble into, as well as a number of propensities that only Arabs have. Who knows? I may just make you smile as you come to a paragraph that describes your Uncle Saleh or Tante Amira down to their striped shirt or metallic nail polish (respectively).

So whether you've already grown up and seen it all, or are just now feeling the effects of a recent (or not) move, this book is for you.

My best wishes go out to everyone who's shed a tear for their old life, or maybe for the life they've just escaped from. God's blessings to you, and may you find what you need—both in life and in this book!

Introduction

What do you picture when you think of the "Middle East?"

Shimmering sands shifting about ancient tombs and a stonescape as old as time? Exotic foods that tempt the palate (and the eyes!)? Maybe even a half-filled cafe, complete with water pipes, Turkish coffee and a belly dancer?

You'd be correct in any of these (if your imagination supplied the same sorts of examples that I just did, you're probably an Arab or Arab American), but chances are that a very different image just flitted behind your eyelids (if you're a non-Arab or Westerner, anyway).

Not very shocking, considering recent events. But not very welcome, if you happen to be the one wearing the tag of "Arab."

This book isn't a *How to Understand Arabs* guide, a *How to Spot a Terrorist Who Happens to Speak Arabic* textbook, nor is it a *History of the Arab Nations* primer.

Rather, it's an attempt to shed some light on the struggles that Arab Americans commonly face. It's my hope that they may find answers to their concerns, solace in the fact that others have them (and maybe a laugh or two, especially if their attitude about becoming American is "been there, done that.").

In fact, my aims for this book are:

1. To assist **first-generation Arab Americans** in the quest for their personal identity (by letting them see that the way they've grown up is much more widespread than they, themselves, may have felt, and by offering solutions to them and their families).

2. To inform **first-, second-and third-generation Arab Americans** who haven't had much exposure to their cultural heritage.

3. To assist **recent immigrants** from Arabic-speaking nations in their acculturation into America (by again pointing out that the plight of the Arab American isn't restricted merely to *them*, and offering solutions and resources).

4. To assist **Arabs who are considering a move** to America, enlightening them about pros and cons they would do well to consider before taking the plunge (maybe they had no idea of the problems or differences associated with raising kids or going to a non-Arab's house for dinner).

5. To assist **Americans** and **other Westerners** who live with/love/are friends with recent immigrants and other Arab-Americans—(this will introduce the non-Arab to the Arab and Arab American behaviors, humor, personality, etc—allowing him or her to achieve better communication through greater understanding). I'd like to point out (yet again) that this book will make the most sense to those who are at least somewhat familiar with Arab culture, but that even Westerners should be able to get more than a glimmer or two of the juxtaposition between East and West.

So, whether you're reading this for yourself or for assistance in dealing with a friend who has ties to the Arab world, happy reading. Just make sure to keep the following in mind:

- Names and identifying details have been changed to protect privacy.

- You may notice an Egyptian viewpoint in this book, extending to the spelling of Arabic words, as well as the actual words I've elected to use (I *did* mention that my family's from Alexandria, didn't I?). You may (especially if you don't actually speak Arabic) also not get some examples the first time around; I have, however, attempted to explain them in such a way that even a non-Arab can understand it.

- Online sources and websites cited here are great resources—but going to Google or Yahoo can give you loads more information than I have room for here, and so can the publications mentioned in the literature review at the back of the book.

- As with any publication concerning cultural studies and the Middle East, there are many things that are debatable now, and will still be 100 years from now—don't get hung up on labels!

Prologue: Words to Live By

Ok, so these words and names aren't necessary for living to a ripe old age or for preventing liver disease, but they may be helpful to take note of before actually jumping in.

Cities—Egyptian

Alexandria
Aswan
Asiut/Asyut
Beni Mazar
Cairo
El Menya/El Minya
Heliopolis
Ismaaliya
Port Saiid
Saiid/The Saiid (Upper Egypt)

Cities—Miscellaneous

Aleppo (*Syria*)
Beirut (*Lebanon*)
Damascus (*Syria*)
Jeddah (*Saudi Arabia*)
Makkah/Mecca (*Saudi Arabia*)
Marrakech (*Morocco*)
Ramallah (*Palestine*)
Riyadh (*Saudi Arabia*)
Tripoli (*Lebanon, Libya*)

Arabic Performers

Abdel Halim Hafez (S., Eg.)
Abdulmajeed Abdullah (S.)
Adel Imam (A., Eg.)

Amr Diab (S., Eg.)
Cheb Khaled (S.)
Cheb Mami (S.)
Ehab Tawfiq (S., Eg.)
Elissa (S.)
Fayza Ahmed (S.)
Haifa Wahby (S.)
Kazem el Saher (S.)
Khalid Agag (S., Eg.)
Mostafa Amar (S., Eg.)
Nancy Agram (S.)
Nawal al Zoghby (S.)
Omm Kalsoum (S., Eg.)
Ragheb Alama (S.)
Samira Saiid (S.)

Legend: A. = Actor; Eg. = Egyptian; S. = Singer

Section One: *Before We Jump to the Fun Stuff, We'll Have to Get Some Groundwork Out of the Way...*

1

What Is An Arab, Anyway?

Picture this: Three attractive guys walk into a bar. One starts chatting with the woman behind the counter. "He's Moroccan, I'm Saudi, and this fella over here, he's from Iran." The bartender smiles politely, waiting for the punchline. When it doesn't appear, she flashes a smile and says, "I've always had a thing for Arabs. Which one of you stunners will buy me my first drink of the evening?" The Saudi slams his open palm onto the bar, almost yelling "They're not Arabs!!"

Melodramatic, I know, but he's right. Going by the most literal of definitions, they're not actually Arabs. So, how does the scenario end? It doesn't matter. But, judging from the fact that at least two Arabic-speakers were present, I'd wager that the waitress got an earful about Arabs, labeling, and the beauty of the Arabic language. (But more on loquaciousness and lecturing later.).

Definition of an Arab

For our purposes, any person from the 300 million whose origins lie in the 22 Arabic-speaking nations of Algeria, Bahrain, Comoros, Djibouti, Egypt, Iraq, Jordan, Kuwait, Lebanon, Libya, Mauritania, Morocco, Oman, Palestine, Qatar, Saudi Arabia, Somalia, Sudan, Syria, Tunisia, United Arab Emirates and Yemen will be called an Arab. But the baby boy born in Tripoli to French parents is *French*, so long as he wasn't actually raised in Tripoli.

Forgotten to us will be the *Arabian debate*, (which wonders whether Saudis are the only actual Arabs—our friend from the last section obviously endorses it!), the *Cross debate* (which ponders whether any Christians *can* be Arabs, especially the Chaldeans and Copts) and any debate between. That's an affirmative—we really *are* doing what political correctness begs us not to—we're going to lump everyone together...for now.

Some people believe that *all* Moslems are Arabs and vice versa, but this is a huge generalization and quite incorrect, on both counts. Yes, most Arabs are

Moslems. No, most Moslems *aren't* Arabs. For example, Iranian and Turkish Moslems aren't Arabs, though much of Arabic culture is derived from Islamic ways, causing Iran and Turkey to share (sort of) in Arab culture, albeit in a different tongue. (Their food is just as delicious, though!).

So, just for today, an Arab is a person who hails from an Arabic-speaking nation, regardless of religion.

That means that I, an American-born, Evangelical Protestant Egyptian, am an Arab.

Definition of a Recent Immigrant

Now that we've finished with the countries involved, let's turn our attention to the length of stay in the United States (or wherever). Obviously, someone who moved to the States 30 years ago wouldn't count as a recent immigrant, regardless of the extent of assimilation that he or she had undergone (or lack thereof). So, the title "recent immigrant," for our purposes, will mean Arabs who have relocated to the States during the past five years, no matter how well they can speak English, get dates or bake apple pie.

Definition of a First-Gen American

Obviously, "First-Gen" is short for "First Generation American," but for the sake of brevity, let's stick with the former. A First-Gen is a person who was born in the United States, regardless of age. Maybe that nice lady down the street is 47 and has an accent that could curl wallpaper. No matter, if she was born in the States, she's a First-Gen.

In fact, for our purposes, anyone who immigrated before kindergarten could count as one. By the way, the term "First-Generation American" can apply to a person of any nationality, not just those of the Arabic persuasion. But when *I* say "First-Gen," you'll know I'm talking about the nationalities that understand *"Ahlan wasahlan."*

Definition of an Arab American

Finally, we come to the nomenclature that identifies us as what we are. For our purposes, an Arab American will be anyone who has a tie to the Arab world—whether born and raised there, or born and raised in America—and who lives in America. So Jessie, a half-Lebanese beauty who has never traveled outside of America, is an Arab American. So is Tamer, who spent his first 31 years in Egypt and just moved to Texas. So am I.

Demographics

Zogby International's data from 2000 reveals the following breakdown of the 3 million Arab Americans by nationality:

> Lebanese—47%
>
> Syrian—15%
>
> Egyptian—9%
>
> Palestinian—6%
>
> Iraqi—3%
>
> Jordanian—2%
>
> Other—18%

I take issue with the estimate of only 3 million—the number is entirely too low. Two reasons for this are *ignorance* and *classification issues*.

The *ignorance* argument doesn't require much explanation; people mark the wrong answer when census time rolls around, whether because their immigrant parents or grandparents kept their lineage a secret, or because the Arab American child was orphaned and/or adopted, causing him or her to also have no idea of their rich heritage.

Moving on, we hit a few *classification issues* that hearken back to the First Wave (1875-1925) of immigrants: On one hand, a family may have hit Australia or Europe before having immigrated to the U.S., immigration laws being such that the people would have been listed as Australian or European, since that's where they had just come from. On the other hand, however, sometimes the Arabs *did* come straight to America—only to be listed as Turks, not Arabs.

In the same set of data as before, Zogby presents another breakdown of Arab Americans—this time by religion:

- *Catholics*, including Roman Catholics, Greek Catholics (Melkites) and Maronites—42%

- *Orthodox*, including Antiochian, Syrian, Greek, and Coptic—23%

- *Moslems*, including Sunni, Shiite, and Druze—23%
- *Protestants*, including the Evangelical Church of Egypt—12%

2

Religion

Arabs often come to America for her religious freedom, but also because of the fact that they can get away with freedom *from* religion…

Let's have a look at the various religions and denominations that thrive—or at least exist—in the Middle East.

Islam

Now called the fastest growing religion in America—and the world—Islam began in the seventh century. The holy text is the Koran, and Moslems look to the *Hadith* (Traditions of the Prophet), believe The Six Articles of Faith, and follow The Five Pillars of Islam.

The Five Pillars of Islam

1—**Faith**: An understanding, belief and recitation of the *Shahada* (which literally translates to "attesting" or "affirmation") in front of a witness is all that's required to create a Moslem. In Arabic, it says "*Ashhadu Alla Ilaha Illa Allah Wa Ashhadu Anna Mohammad Rasulu Allah,*" which is translated to mean, "I bear witness that there is no deity other than Allah, and that Mohammad is his servant and Messenger." There are actually three sub-points of the *Shahada* that aren't as widely known to non-Moslems—

Point 1: *Tauhid-ar-Rububiyya* (that Allah is the Creator of all),
Point 2: *Tauhid-al-Uluhiyya* (that only Allah has the right to be worshipped) and
Point 3: *Tauhid-al-Asma was-Sifat* (that the names and descriptions of Allah are all true).

2—Salah: Five times a day (dawn, noon, mid-afternoon, sunset and night-fall), Moslems all over the world fulfill this second Pillar, whose name translates into "prayer." While the actual prayers, comprised of Koranic verses, are said in Arabic, supplications may be said in the native tongue of the faithful.

The *Adhan* (Call to Prayer) translates into:

God is most great. (x4)
I testify that there is no god except God. (x2)
I testify that Mohammad is the messenger of God. (x2)
Come to prayer! (x2, turning the face right)
Come to success! (x2, turning the face left)
Prayer is better than sleep (x2, recited only in the prayer at dawn)
God is most great. (x2)
There is no god except God. (x1)

3—Zakat: The Arabic word for "purification" and "growth," *Zakat* refers to almsgiving. The percentage is 2.5%, calculated on a person's entire wealth and assets, rather than their salary. Above and beyond this there is *Sadaqa*, or "voluntary charity," which doesn't have to be financial, and includes giving a friendly smile. *Sadaqa* should be done in secret.

4—Sawm: The Arabic word for "fasting," this pillar directs the Moslem to keep from food, drink, and sexual relations, beginning at sunup and ending at sundown during every day of the month of *Ramadan*. This is done to keep the person sympathetic to the poor around him, and close to Allah.

5—Hagg: For those in good health and able to afford it, the pilgrimage to Mecca during the twelfth month in the Islamic calendar is the final obligation.

Contrary to popular Western thought, Moslems do not hate Jesus, nor do they disbelieve in his miracles and the Virgin Birth—they just don't see Him as the son of God, as Christians do. And contrary to yet another patently American fear, all Moslems are not terrorists (most aren't!). In fact, to my knowledge, there isn't one single religion in all the world whose goal is to kill people.

In my experience, Moslems are some of the nicest people to walk the earth (especially Arab Moslems). Their gregarious friendliness, generosity, kindness, and devotion to their religion set them apart. In college, I would spend the hours between midnight and dawn in either the university Cybercafe or lounge, together with three or four Moslem exchange students I knew. We began every evening with "So, how're you doing, man?" but would soon shift to the serious stuff: They would ask me all the questions about Christianity that no one back home could—or would—answer. I, of course, asked them all the questions I had, too. No subject was taboo—we discussed our religions' respective takes on the West, morality, salvation, Jesus, terrorism, sacraments.

Those conversations ran the gamut of both religions, and I'll treasure them always. The most precious moment that I remember came one night, when everyone was getting up to leave. I had just gotten a cappuccino and *didn't* feel like getting up, and began shaking hands with everyone who had been there, apart from Sam, a Persian Moslem friend of mine who hadn't moved from his seat. When he started talking, his topic of choice was the same one that a girl had brought up earlier: prayer. I had asked Sam if Moslems loved God or respected him, and he had answered, "It's not our place to love him, and we're not worthy of it." That had troubled me, because I thought, how can you talk to God so much and not grow to love Him?

He answered that they didn't talk to God the way he'd heard me talking to God: the whole "*Dear God. Thanks for everything that You've given us, thanks for loving us, thanks for keeping us safe and please watch over us. Draw us nearer to You and may we love others more and help others to love You more. Forgive us for our sins and thanks again for being so wondrous, beautiful, generous, loving—thanks for being You! And for giving us the chance to know You. In Your precious name we pray, Amen.*"

He explained how *his* prayers went (from the Koran's first Sura, "*In the name of God, Most Gracious, Most Merciful. Praise be to God, Lord of the universe. Most Gracious, Most Merciful. Master of the Day of Judgment. You alone we worship; You alone we ask for help. Guide us in the right path; the path of those whom You blessed; not of those who have deserved wrath, nor of the strayers.*") and I thought "Oh." Maybe I've always had a need to express myself in a creative way that was uniquely me (I have), but I was as baffled at the ritualism that Sam described as I am with the formulaic nature of the prayers of Catholics and Orthodox Christians. But that all changed when he leaned back, stretching, hands behind his head, and smiled contentedly, like a cat. "But Sally," he said, heavily-accented words lilting around his deep, melodious voice, "if only you knew how I feel after prayers—it's…it's like the feeling you get after a shower. Clean and refreshed. Ready for anything."

I can't tell you how much that changed my perception of—well, not just Islam, but all religions. It created a tolerance in me that had never been there before. It made me think that, despite all of the differences, there was beauty in all religions, even if I didn't see it or couldn't understand it. (That all changed when I attended a conference that encouraged Moslem-Christian brotherhood since "we all believe the same thing under different names, anyway." That irked me, I have to admit. Friendship, peace and love between the faiths is fine and well, but at least call a spade a spade. Islam and Christianity differ on many points, and that's okay. No one said that we all have to believe the same thing in order to be friends, did they? Because if so, I'd be out of about 97 percent of my friends.).

Everything you've read here (up until my spiel about Moslems being nice, anyway) is agreed upon by the two main branches of Islam—the *Shiite* (also called *Shia)* and the *Sunni*, whose differences lie in the politics and history surrounding the Prophet Mohammed's successor.

Another group of Moslems—albeit Moslems who aren't actually recognized as such—are the *Mowahhidoon*, more commonly known as the *Druze*. This sect does not adhere to the Five Pillars, and counts the Koran as only one-sixth of their holy text, called *Kitab il Hikma* (Book of Wisdom). Author B.A. Robinson sketches this portrait of the Druze's exclusivity:

> After the death of their leader Baha al-Din in 1031 CE, their religion became exclusive: they do not accept converts; they do not marry outside their faith. They do not leave the faith. They currently total about 200 to 300 thousand members. The Druze keep their religion secret, and often pose as members of the locally dominant religion.

So, while the Druze would never be called "pure" Moslems, they share more with Islam than with Christianity (just ask pollsters Zogby International), though some would argue that the Druze are neither Christian nor Moslem.

Christianity

Christians were the majority in the Arab world until the seventh century, when Islam began to spread. After that came debates over religion and freedom, over church and state. As can be expected, a number of civil not-exactly-wars were fought, including the 1911 Moslem vs. Copt debacle in Egypt, and the 1933 massacre of hundreds of Iraqi Christians—and that's just the beginning.

It's really no surprise, then, that many Christian Arabs who felt persecuted and restricted back home have made their way to the United States in search of the religious freedom that this nation was founded for. In fact, The Arab American Institute cites that 77 percent of Arab Americans are Christians.

Christianity, by the way, has many denominations, as we'll soon find out, but the basic tenets are the same: a belief that the Father, Son and Holy Spirit all exist in one person (the Holy Trinity), the belief and admission that Jesus, the Son of God, was crucified to save humanity from sin (and that we could never save ourselves anyway), and finally, a repentance from the aforementioned sin.

There are a few twists, though. The Evangelicals, a rather new addition to Christianity, believe that a person is saved through faith alone, while the Orthodox Church, which lays claim to being the first Christian church ever, maintains that good works *are* necessary—much like the Catholic Church's teachings. (A Protestant would fire back that works *are* important, in that true faith is characterized by works, but that the works alone are basically worth nothing without the faith.).

The Middle East Council of Churches (MECC) counts the following Churches as *Evangelical*: The Evangelical Church of Egypt (Synod of the Nile), Episcopal Church in the Sudan, The Evangelical Church in Sudan, Evangelical Lutheran Church in Jordan, The Synod of the Evangelical Church of Iran, National Evangelical Synod of Syria and Lebanon, The National Evangelical Union of Lebanon, The Presbyterian Church in the Sudan, The Union of the Armenian Evangelical Churches in the Near East, Protestant Church in Algeria, Eglise Reformée de France en Tunisie, The National Evangelical Church in Kuwait and finally, The Episcopal Church in Jerusalem and the Middle East, under which fall The Diocese of Egypt, The Diocese of Jerusalem, Jordan, Syria and Lebanon, The Diocese of Cyprus and the Gulf, and The Diocese of Iran.

The *Catholic Churches* belonging to the MECC are the Armenian Catholic Church of Cilicia, The Chaldean Catholic Church of Babylon, Greek Melkite Catholic Patriarchate of Antioch, Alexandria & Jerusalem, The Maronite Church of Antioch, Syrian Catholic Church of Antioch, The Coptic Catholic Church of Alexandria and The Latin Patriarchate of Jerusalem. With the exception of the last one mentioned, each of these churches belongs to the *Eastern Rite*, which has ties to the Roman Catholic church.

Finally, come the *Orthodox* churches—The Greek Orthodox Church of Alexandria and All Africa, The Greek Orthodox Church of Antioch and All the East, The Greek Orthodox Church of Jerusalem, The Greek Orthodox Church of Cyprus—and the *Oriental Orthodox* Churches—The Armenian Apostolic Church, Catholicosate of Cilicia, The Syrian Orthodox Church of Antioch and All the East and my *personal* favorite, The Coptic Orthodox Church, which I attend—much to the chagrin of my militantly Protestant family. The Coptic

Mass is especially beautiful, with chants in Qibti, the language of the pharaohs. (But more on Copts in just a minute).

Native Christians

We've already discussed the spread of Islam in the seventh century, but let's have a closer look at the following groups of Christian "Arabs" whose bloodlines weren't affected by the Arabs.

Chaldeans

If you've gone to Sunday school even twice, chances are that you're (perhaps unknowingly) familiar with the Chaldeans. After all, it was this Aramaic tribe who brought us King Nebuchadnezzar, back in 1100ish B.C.—yes, the one who tried to execute Shadrach, Meshach and Abednego when they refused to worship a statue he'd built. The very same Nebuchadnezzar, in fact, who went on to build one of the Seven Wonders of the World, the Hanging Gardens of Babylon.

These people indirectly contributed a great deal to religion, since Abraham (from Ur of the Chaldees) was forefather to Mohammed, Moses and Jesus, who each played large roles in Islam, Judaism and Christianity, respectively. The Chaldeans more directly contributed to civilization, ranging from philosophy, art and literature to their mathematical achievements, such as the use of decimals, zeros, and instruments that *measured* (sundials and other pre-clockish gadgets) and *recorded* (calendars) the passage of time. In my book, however, their two greatest accomplishments lay in their invention of the wheel and in their eventual language, Aramaic (which made their prior language, Akkadian, obsolete).

Aramaic, which is sometimes called Chaldean, originated in Babylon. This ancient language uses a 22-letter alphabet that actually laid the groundwork for two other languages that arose later on—Arabic and Hebrew. What I find fascinating (if you can feel "fascinating" up your spine) is that the language is over 2000 years old—and the Chaldeans still use it today!

Much like the *Fos'ha* (classical) and *'Aama* (everyday slangish) Arabic that are used in Islam and daily life (respectively), the classical form of Aramaic is used liturgically, whereas a more everyday version is used, well, every day. So—if our earlier definition of being a native Arabic speaker *or* coming from a land whose official language is Arabic makes one an Arab, then the Chaldeans are sort-of Arabs, since they *do* come from Mesopotamia (modern-day Iraq), whose official language is Arabic.

By the way, one of the more famous Aramaic-speakers in history was Jesus—even more fascinating!

Copts

Another group of native Christians who still get to use their native language in the Arab world—over 2000 years later—is the Copts. Copts are native Egyptians, the largest group of Christians in the Arab world, the most undiluted descendants of the pharaonic people. Unfortunately, most of us don't have the luxury of speaking Coptic (*Qibti* is the Arabic word for it) in everyday life—in fact, relatively few Copts can even read and write the language, and even fewer can speak it, though there has been an underground resurgence (of late) dedicated to bringing the language back, complete with newsgroups, mailing lists and websites.

Rather, those of us who are Coptic Orthodox (or attend the Coptic Orthodox mass, anyway) get to hear this beautiful language in the liturgy. Maybe I'm biased—actually, I know I am—but this is a hundred steps up from fascinating. This is hearing the same exact language that the last of the pharaohs spoke. These are the same songs and chants that the ancient Egyptians chanted. Just think—even the *melodies* are over 2000 years old! (I believe I may have mentioned something about being biased?).

Another thing that I mentioned a few minutes back is that modern-day Copts are the most undiluted descendents of the pharaonic people, who were the original Copts. This refers to the fact that the Arab invaders who brought Islam to Egypt were obviously non-Egyptian and non-Coptic, and furthermore, to the fact that the subsequent intermarriage with their converts, and the settling of these interracial families into Egypt, made for increasingly thinned ties to Coptic forefathers as generations passed.

The first time I heard this, I theorized that there had to have been *some* further intermarriage between the purer still-Copts and those who had converted to Islam, but my friend Hany set me straight: "If that were the case," he began, "the family would automatically have had to become Moslem. Hence, those who remain Copts to this day refused to convert and thus have no Moslem ancestry or blood." Dr. Edwin Wakin, author of *A Lonely Minority: the Modern Story of Egypt's Copts*, concurs, estimating that up to 80 percent of the current Moslem population in Egypt carry the Coptic lineage in the beginnings of their family trees.

In terms of the Coptic Orthodox faith, it came into being as a result of St. Mark and his extensive teachings of Christianity in Egypt. Dr. Wakin further enlightens us about the ancient Egyptians, telling us how "*Christianity...appealed to them with its clear-cut morality and assurance of life after death, with which Egyptians have always been preoccupied...The Coptic religion [Orthodoxy] has been diluted by heavy doses of superstition...the content of Coptic life has become part Pharaonic, part Christian, part oriental, part petit bourgeois.*"

In terms of the origin of the word "Copt," Christian Cannuyer, in the English translation of his *Coptic Egypt—The Christians of the Nile*, has this to say about the Coptic name, among other things:

> The Copts are the Christians of Egypt. Theirs is among the most ancient forms of Christianity, born in the time of Jesus. The name derives from the Arabic *Qibt*, an abbreviation of the Greek name *Aigyptios* (Egyptian); this in turn is a derivation of *Hikuptah*, House of the Energy of Ptah, the religious name for Memphis, the capital city of ancient Egypt. Coptic Christianity mingles remnants of pharaonic practices, elements of Hellenistic and Byzantine Egyptian culture, and the dynamism of Arab civilization.

Perhaps he should have said "Coptic *Orthodoxy*" rather than Christianity, since there are now branches of Catholicism and Protestantism in Egypt. Nevertheless, as in Cannuyer's words above, the term "Coptic" is, more often than not, misused to denote those Egyptians of the Orthodox faith, though the most accurate modern usage of the word would be "Egyptian Christians." The aforementioned Dr. Wakin takes it a step further, stating that "*in the Coptic language, "Copts" means "people of Egypt" and the Copts use the term literally, referring to themselves as the "true Egyptians."*"

Perhaps it's this fact that has made the Copts so persecuted, or maybe it's their tenacity in clinging to Christianity. Either way, the Copts are one of the most put-upon people of the Middle East. In yet another gem by the very perceptive and articulate Dr. Wakin, we see that in "*any minority, its symbol is a badge in times of prosperity, a brand in times of trouble.*" This may refer to the ever-present symbol of the cross, as in those that they imprint into the walls of their houses, as in the pendants that they always wear, the icons that they hang, the tattoos that they wear at their wrists, even the sign of the cross that they make when worried, scared or grateful. It could also refer to the fact that Copts are forced to state their religious affiliation on all official documents—not unlike the Star of David during the Holocaust, or the Mark of the Beast/Seals of the Righteous in the book of Revelations.

But despite the killing of 144,000 Copts (a friend tells me that the figure's actually well over 800,000) between 303 and 311—killing that was sanctioned by then-emperor Diocletian (interesting to note that the beginning of the Coptic Orthodox's Year of the Martyrs falls on September 11th)—despite the 1320 razing of every Coptic church in Egypt by Moslem fanatics, despite the more recent and gratuitous rash of murders (1200 Copts in Egypt have fallen since 1992), despite persecution in the streets, in the workplace (Copts can almost never make it to the highest level of any job), by the government (the president himself must issue a decree before a church can be built or even repaired) and all of the other travesties and tragedies that I don't have the space to recount, the Copts live on—upwards of six million strong!—both ethnically and religiously.

In a final snippet by the informative and illustrious Dr. Wakin (I promise!), we find a commentary on—and tribute to—the strength of the people that the Pharaohs and their kingdoms would have been more than proud to call their descendants:

> Unlike the American Indians, the Copts have not practically disappeared under the sword of outsiders who conquered and settled; nor did they absorb and assimilate the invaders as did the Chinese. Unlike Armenians and Jews, the Copts have had little migration and no diaspora. It is both their burden and their fortune to have had only one home—the Nile Valley.

3

Arab Views On Everyday Things

Just to make sure you and I are on the same page concerning the Arab personality, let's run through the basics:

Religious Devotion

Arabs view life with a sort of fatalism, choosing prayers and *"inshallah"* (if God wills it) to worry and heartache. And if something bad *does* happen—*"maalish"* ("it's ok" or "never mind"), because God knows best and allowed it.

One thing that Christians and Moslems wholeheartedly agree on is piousness, which is admired in any form and, in fact, considered to be a redeeming quality in the face of any lesser quality. Piety and devoutness are displayed when a person liberally sprinkles many *"inshallah"*s, *"alhamdulilah"*s, *"allah yi barkak"*s, and *"rabinah maak"*s into conversation, and also when a person offers to pray for another. Atheism, however, paints a person as a black-hearted individual, as attested to by the disparaging remarks *"Ah, ya kafir!"* ("Oh, you unbeliever!") or *"Inta mitaarafsh rabinah!"* ("You don't know God!").

Pride

The Arabic sense of pride is the most difficult facet there is to deal with—for the ignorant and uninitiated, as well as for the Arabs who have done the offending and have to live with the consequences, actually. This is because of the Arab's inherent regard for one's self-esteem, honor, dignity, and reputation. This is what also causes Arabs to sometimes be a bit on the touchy side—and I don't mean the "free with your hands" kind, either.

Arabs can—and do!—put on a long face (*"yilwo booz-hom"*) when confronted with real or imagined slights to their pride. Too brief of a farewell, too many days without communication or unchecked remarks of a catty nature, even, can linger in an Arab's mind for weeks, only to be brought up later, in the midst of a seemingly unrelated argument (or out of the blue, for that matter). This is not to call the world population of Arabs paranoid, just…a bit prickly at times.

For this reason, it's generally best to employ a great amount of tact when they ask you to "give it to me straight" and "tell it like it is"—if not, you might find yourself heaped with "friendly constructive criticism"—which you may not find friendly in the least! (I can tell you this because it's happened to me countless times.).

Another tactic that Arabs may sometimes come up with is telling a few little white ones in order to "save face." A common example of this is that when a suitor expresses interest in a young lady and suddenly backs away after a few days, the girl oftentimes mentions (to everyone within earshot!) how sweet and kind the guy is—if it weren't, alas, for the egregious way his ears stuck out, the way he walked, or the fact that his father went bald at 37. Keep in mind that she has no idea why he's backed off, but wants to look as though the shunning was *her* idea. This way, if he "comes to his senses" and tries again, she looks as though she's doing *him* a service, and if he stays away, she can always pretend that she was afraid for her future sons' hairlines.

But the Arab sense of pride isn't only associated with arguments and lies and the like—not by a long shot. Rather, it's this sense of pride and living up to one's image that causes Arabic-speaking parents to push their children into studying diligently, protecting their reputations and dressing well. How does pride equate with fashion, you may ask? I'll tell you…

Dressing well is very important to Arabs, not so much for the sake of stopping the opposite gender in their tracks, but because of their self-image/-esteem/-respect, as well as pride in their appearance—after all, they reason, why dress in polyester when you can afford the silk? And more so, why look less rich than you are?

That's why it's not uncommon to see women at the market decked out in metallic eye-shadow and sequined tops, or Arabic men in thoroughly pricey but thoroughly hideous shirts with scary prints all over them. That's also why some women, especially from the Saiid (Upper Egypt) are (in)famous for wearing every piece of jewelry that they own—at once!

The men are also very fond of jewelry, wearing bracelets, watches, cuff links, pins and heavy chains (some crosses I've seen Lebanese men wearing make rappers look unadorned and plain). Their love of luxury and showing off causes them to invest in other such embellishments as money clips, fountain pens, lighters and cigarette cases in fashion forward precious metals, although Moslem men aren't supposed to wear gold and instead stick to Islamically-correct metals, such as platinum or silver.

This reminds me of my college days, when I knew a guy who wore more jewelry than I did; he was a Saudi who was never seen without his trademark sterling ring, watch, ID bracelet, and 12 mm curb-link necklace. On the other hand, I met my friend's fiancé—a Palestinian Moslem—when I was in graduate school and *he* told me that he didn't wear any jewelry at all because his family interpreted the Koran to restrict the actual institution of adornment, not just the metal.

In rounding out the fashion section of this chapter, let me provide you with a formula for determining whether an Arab you are meeting for the first time is or isn't a recent immigrant—the more sparkly and outrageous the outfit, the less time they've spent off the boat.

Temperament and Histrionics

The temperament of Arabs should be very interesting to Americans, given how different the East and West are. Instead, however, is a rather amusing pattern of Americans' being taken aback when they witness the relative unruliness, for lack of a better word, of Arabic communication.

Gulf countries aside, Arabs have been known to yell, prance, hiss, wail, chortle, point fingers, gesticulate wildly and dance about in their efforts to make a point. Obviously, not every single Arab in the entire world does this, but none of these behaviors would cause a hush to fall over a gathering that the "hysterical" person was disturbing. Emotion is almost expected and sincerity shown through repetition, raised voices and a passionate delivery, though some may argue that in more educated and/or Westernized circles, this blatantly Arabic display is anomalous and bothersome.

Despite an Arab's most fervent attempts to preserve the façade of a "happy home" when in public, the occasional skirmish *can* take place. I was once very amused to witness an Egyptian family trying to decide between Outback Steakhouse and The Olive Garden. The father and son were raising their voices at one another while the mother and daughter exchanged embarrassed glances. The overtly distressed mother finally put a hand on her husband's arm. "Enough already! Stop fighting and yelling!" she screeched. The men concurrently turned to her and yelled—"We're not yelling!"

Adding to this sense of melodrama are sweeping hand-gestures and the colorful aphorisms that are so common in the Arabic language. For example, every time a female friend of the Arabic persuasion notices a new ring on my hand, she hits me with "*ha'tom ra'bitik!*" and "*ha nott fi kirshik!,*" which can be interchanged with another phrase they always say to me when they've heard I just went shopping—"*ha mawitik!*" (literally, "I'll kill you!" My mother wants to "kill me" for repeating these less-than-classy phrases, by the way).

Another mechanism of the Arabic communication system is making a great show of things, whether in the midst of an argument (as in the example above) or in normal conversation, as documented by phrases like "*battalo da wi'ssmaaoo da!*" which translates to "everyone stop and listen to this!"

Appealing to strangers is another phenomenon that semi-frequently appears. During a party, someone may call across the room for backup: "Ahmed! Come here and tell Fawzy that I did NOT eat two pizzas!"

Language

The Arabic language is one of the most beautiful languages in the world, and Arabic-speakers it won't let you forget it! Formal, written Arabic is called *Fos'ha*, and the slangy "everyday" variety *Aama*.

Fos'ha has barely changed in 1000 years and remains consistent from Morocco, the African treasure, to Egypt, the Jewel of the Nile, all the way to Jordan, the Gulf States and Iraq. It's used for essays and speeches and the Koran, but rarely used in conversation. In fact, some Arabs never even bother learning it—Arab American kids certainly don't (usually).

Aama differs from country to country, village to village, and family to family, even. The differences don't just lie in the accent and pronunciation, but in the actual words used. As a child, I was always baffled by tales revealing how the Lebanese called a car "*sayara*" and a tomato "*bandura.*" After all, everyone knew that a car was really a "*arabaya*" and a tomato a "*tamatmaya!*" Upon maturity, I was scandalized to find that what I had considered to be the word for "tomato" was actually a Western fabrication! I have since learned that some Egyptians call the red vegetable *oota,* and given up on salads altogether.

Thanks to Egypt's booming film industry and the miracle of satellite technology, Egyptian Arabic is understood by many—if not most—Arabic-speakers, although Egyptians may not be able to follow every dialect that they come into contact with.

I found this out the hard way when I spent a week forcing all of the Egyptians in town to listen to Sting's hit *Desert Rose,* which featured Algerian singer Cheb Mami. None of them could understand his words, although they *did* understand him perfectly when he sang with Samira Saiid in another duet, "Youm Wara Youm" ("Day after day"). The Egyptians and I deduced that his accent had morphed owing to the fact that he was singing with a singer (Samira) who was a Moroccan-born honorary Egyptian. We also noticed that Cheb Khaled, a Tunisian singer, sounded much more decipherable in his duet of "Alby" ("My heart") with Egyptian megastar Amr Diab.

Despite the fact that the Arab world is rather keen on Egyptian Arabic, it must be understood that Arabs each pride themselves on their own dialects, and take an even greater pride in having a mastery of more than one dialect. This is very understandable, considering the fact that some dialects are as dissimilar from one another as the English and Russian languages are. For this reason, then, one might guess that the average Arab was repulsed by the non-Arab's attempts to learn Arabic. Not so.

Immigrants and First-Generation Arab-Americans alike are warmed to hear people making an effort to say *ahlan* or *inshallah*, and go as far as teaching their most-used phrases to those around them. In fact, an Egyptian lady I know has taught the words "*zift*" and "*aasal*" to every person she works with (the former is a slangy way to say "bad" and the latter to say "sweet" or "good," though the actual translations are "tar" and "honey," respectively). She maintains that it's easier to teach them the words than to cast about for their English translations when she's trying to be witty. Arabs and Arab-Americans alike are usually delighted to meet other Arabic-speakers, either in a market, religious gathering or online.

This delight in their own language extends to the media, as well. When an Egyptian-American hears a song by Abdel Halim Hafez or Amr Diab, an immediate sense of bliss arises. The same goes for Iraqi-Americans and Kazem el Saher, Lebanese-Americans (or any red-blooded Arabic-speaking woman) and Ragheb Alama, and Saudi-Americans and Abdel Majeed Abdullah.

One very nice 40-something Christian Moroccan-American lady I had the pleasure of meeting over dinner told me, in perfect and heavily-accented English, that America was her home because it had given her the freedom that her mother country hadn't. She literally spent about 25 minutes going on about how she had no good memories of Marrakech, how she was glad that she'd come to America as a teenager. But tears sprang to her eyes when Abdel Halim's *Sawah* came on the restaurant's hi-fi.

In terms of communicating, Arabs love to hear themselves speak, and are always proud of an articulate conversation, speech, essay, not to mention an especially clever joke or anecdote—even if it's par for the course. (Arab American writers have sometimes been accused of being folksy or cliché, but this is an admired trait among Arabs, who love a good tale, and a well told one, especially.)

Arab Americans quite frequently fall into a pattern of speaking a hybrid of English and Arabic, sometimes mixing it up as much as 70/30, depending on their mood and the person with whom they're speaking. In fact, Arabs and especially Arab Americans sometimes come up with totally new words that may become so ingrained in their vocabulary that they have no idea whether the word is an actual Arabic word, a Western fabrication (like the *"tamatmaya"* that you read about earlier), or a word that just "appeared" (from another language, maybe?).

An example of this is the word *salfasha*, which means "selfishness." But is it a real word? Because the word for "selfishness" is actually *"ananaya."* That's not to say that there can't be two words that mean similar things, it's just interesting how the Arabic resembles the English. Other examples of this are *"narvaza,"* which means "nervousness" and sometimes "irritability," among other things, *"mitenshina,"* another way to say "chock-full of tension," and *"mitaqlama,"* the Arabic word for "acclimated." I've heard well-read Arabs debate the validity of this last word's etymology (extensively).

Hearkening back to the bit about redundancy making the case for sincerity, we find several oaths designed to convince people that the speaker is in earnest, although Arabs, being more than a bit religiously-minded, don't mind getting in as many prayers per day as possible. Some oaths are *"wil masiih"* ("By the Messiah"), *"wilnabi"* (By the Prophet), *"walahi"* ("By God"), *"oddam rabinah"* ("Before God"), and *"bi amana"* ("With faithfulness," meaning "honestly").

Superstition

Every culture has its superstitions, and Arabic culture is no exception. Moslems and Christians alike share in this, though the Orthodox are probably the most superstitious of all the Arabic Christians.

One example of Orthodox practices that could count as "superstitious" is the practice of asking a patron saint to help the faithful find something, protect someone, etc. An example of this is the time that my friend Ahlam found a package of hair clips in a store that we were ransacking (during store hours—there was a sale going on, lest you think that poor Ahlam and I were up to no good). The clips were cute and looked expensive and, for some reason, had a 75 percent off tag on them. She couldn't believe her luck, which seemed to fade when she realized that she'd need another package of matching clips—one for each side of her hair. She searched for another few minutes, and I was recruited to join in the hunt. Nothing. Not a glimmer of them.

"Oh, too bad," said I, glancing wistfully at the pizza place next door and not sounding sorry at all. "There's only one thing left to do now," she muttered in rapid-fire Arabic, "Anba Waniss, help me find one," she kept muttering, and I stood back and watched from under sharply raised brows. "Anba Waniss, help me, come on, don't make a liar of me! Anba—look, Sally!" I *was* looking, and saw that she'd found one. I can't say that I'm convinced that Anba Waniss had a role in the affair, but there's no telling *her* that.

The Orthodox also love and greatly revere their Popes, both alive and deceased. In fact, they even believe that some of them can perform miracles—like the Coptic Orthodox Church's late Baba Kyrillos, whose photo can apparently make great things happen. Like the time when Mina, the son of my dear friend, Suzan, lost his wallet. He had been visiting his mother at work one day, when his wallet found its way out of his pocket. He, of course, had no idea. The next day, one of Suzan's friends from work walked up to her and said, "Boy, you Copts sure get around." Suzan smiled beautifully, but had no idea what her friend meant, and asked. "How so?"

Her friend held out a wallet with an unfamiliar photo of Suzan's beloved Baba Kyrillos, and then went back to her desk. Imagine Suzan's surprise when she flipped to the Driver's License section and saw her own son's face looking back at her! That evening, she showed the photo to Mina. "That's a nice one, Mom," he told her. "Did you buy that today?" Instead of answering, she held out his wallet. "This was in there," she informed him, filling him in on the story—"Didn't you know that you'd lost it?"

You probably won't believe me when I tell you that stories like this are not only common, but par for the course; you may even call me a liar if I told you that almost every single Orthodox Copt that I've ever spoken to in my life—whether dear friend or source for this book, whether East Coaster or West, whether Cairo-based or Alexandria-, whether Egyptian-based or Coptic-American—over 90 percent of the hundreds that I know—has, at some point, mentioned Baba Kyrillos to me or told me a similar tale.

Another Orthodox belief is that making the sign of the cross will protect something or someone, like all the times I'm unhappy about being caught in a storm, or worried about going on a long trip and leaving my house alone, or concerned that the mosquito that just bit me was carrying West Nile Virus. Yes, you've guessed it—the friendly members of my local chapter of the Coptic Orthodox Laity inform me that I should make the sign of the cross and everything will be fine. Finally comes the belief that a person who refuses prayer or communion *could* be possessed. There are many other superstitions, by the way, some of which *are* shared by Catholics (although the actual saints differ), and some of which aren't.

In terms of superstitious behavior that's shared by Christian and Moslem Arabs, we find euphemisms and *Hassad*.

In the euphemistic tradition, certain things such as disease, death and hardship are never joked about or directly spoken of. Instead of saying "when I die," an Arab may say *"lemma at'lihid,"* which means "when I get put to sleep."

This euphemistic tendency to dance around the actual word is very common in Arabic culture, such as when a friend of mine called to tell his cousin that his grandmother had passed on:

> *Waguid*—"Hi there."
> *Fahima*—"How's Aunty?"
> *Waguid*—"Well…At least you're well…"

This might not seem too different from Western behavior, although it is when you pair it with the Arab's vehement dismissal of any "After I'm gone" and "I really *do* prefer cremation" talk (and the planning that should go with it). Arab Americans who weren't raised in the Arabic tradition don't display this as much, and Arabs who yearn to be Westernized mightn't, either.

Complimenting someone could get you an accusation of putting *hassad* (envy, but sort of like the evil eye) on them. This could be the reason that people like to compliment in reverse—"Oh Samia, what's with those tiny eyes?" when poor Samia's eyes are actually wide and beautiful. And it's definitely the reason that baby boys in the Saiid have traditionally had their eyes painted with *kohl* (eyeliner that, in Egypt, anyway, sometimes comes packaged in a metal container with a peacock or other figurine, whose arm or leg was the applicator)—so that they would be confused with less important girls and not have a *hassad*-inducing "How wonderful that you have a boy!" thrown at them, possibly killing them.

Tradition

Margaret Nydell, in *Understanding Arabs*, put it like this:

> "How do you compare the relative value of a communications satellite with the wisdom of a village elder? What good is a son who is a computer expert but lacks filial respect? How do you cope with a highly educated daughter who

announces that she never intends to marry?" (I just felt my parents flinch at that last one.)

My grandmother, on the other hand, has her own feelings on the matter—"*Hatis'all il garrab wala tis'all il khabeer?*" This means "Will you ask the experimenter or the experienced?"

As you can see, tradition plays a big part in Middle Eastern culture—both on its own and in terms of almost every other major segment of Arab life. Some of the traditions at the forefront involve religion, marriage, and family.

In terms of religion, everyone has one. People take the religion that they were born into, even if they live their lives as "nominal" (that is, in name only) members of the faith. Conversions and "searching one's soul to find the truth" are relatively rare, especially since a conversion would, at the very *least,* be seen as a betrayal of the family, but might more seriously result in disowning or death.

In terms of marriage, the institution of Arab marriage can sometimes seem to peacefully (sort of) coexist amidst two models: the *Leaning Tower* model (named after the Leaning Tower of Pisa) and the *Big Fat Greek* model.

In the first, the wife asks "How high?" when the King of the Manor hints at jumping. She also keeps her eyes down (some women do, anyway) and wouldn't think of sending hubby to sleep on the sofa even if he's forgotten her birthday or admitted that those jeans *do* make her look fat. This model actually gets its name from a number of spunky, professional Arab-American women who, under differing circumstances and at different times, have enlisted me as a general and engaged in warlike and tearful skirmishes with their spouses. Words were screeched—sometimes by both parties, but often just by him—and that was that.

After Mr. Macho Breadwinner Male had yelled at the wife, appealed to me ("*Saaaaally*! Can you blame me for _____ when she's intent on being so _____?!??!!"), and flounced off in a tizzy, the formerly sassy woman would lock her invariably bloodshot eyes on mine and just *stare* for a moment. Then, we would talk a bit before I made up an excuse to leave ("But really, Salwa, it's important that I call the bank NOW, so that I could lock in a great loan rate for when I buy an andiron collection."). Every single one of the conversations went something like this:

Me: "Why do you put up with that? Why don't you just hit him or yell back or something?"
Them: "Oh, but that's 'ehb (wrong, *haram*, unseemly, etc.). I couldn't."
Me: "Uh, ok..."

Them: "Sally, don't marry an Arab. He'll only end up breaking your spirit. The Arab wife is *"il heta il mayla"* ("the wall that leans") and that will never change."

Not too cheery, eh? On the other hand, however, we finally come across the *Big Fat Greek* model, which actually has nothing to do with stout Athenians and everything to do with the excellent film called *My Big Fat Greek Wedding*, particularly the scene where the heroine, Toula, is lamenting her father's outlawing of college classes. Toula's mother, who is being subjected to the lamentation, informs her daughter that "the man is the head of the house, but the woman is the neck. She can make the head turn *any* way she wants!"

In addition to this bit of sass on the part of some Arabic women, (especially the heroines in Arabic films, like *Anaam,* the wife of Omar Sherif's character in the excellent film "Al Aragoz") there is also a tendency, by spouses, to feign indignance and/or engage in verbal sparring (rent Emma Thompson's version of *Much Ado About Nothing* if you want to witness a Western version of this).

Finally, in terms of tradition and family, we answer to our parents (especially the male one), respect our elders and consider our families—from immediate to third generation twice removed—in every decision we make. Prizes to all the well-read readers who know that this is called *collectivism*.

Collectivism

In years past, psychiatrists in Arab countries made no money. Succinctly put by a friendly Egyptian I met once, "I have God and I have my family—What else do I need?"

As I just mentioned, Arabic families are not made up of free-standing individuals, but *all* of the members, even the ones we've met only twice. We cover up for each other, help each other out, and generally behave the way a family *should.*

Family is so important a concept to Middle Easterners that it's not unusual for cousins—even first cousins—to marry. This happens for two reasons: The first is that one party definitely knows the other party's class, family and upbringing, called *"aslo wi faslo"* in Arabic. The second is that since the prospective spouses are related, they'll have *one* family's interests to consider, not two. Meaning that scheming in-laws would carry less weight in the relationship, and that a divorce would be less likely (Moslems are allowed to divorce, but Christians are strongly discouraged from it).

In the West, missing a day at work could spell the end of a job, but in the Middle East, a job plays second fiddle to the demands of family. *Everything* actually plays second fiddle to family, including choice of spouse, occupation and success in life, though collectivism ensures that the young Arab makes the best choices and therefore has no choice *but* to be successful. This is because the honor of the family is at stake.

In terms of deciding upon a spouse, Arab families take the "She's not good enough for *my* son!" mentality to an extreme. Let's say that young Ahmed wants to marry a nice girl he met at the market. If she turns out to have any shady relatives, the deal's off. If her second cousin died from cancer or suffered from depression, the girl at the market gets the big kiss-off. This is one of the reasons that Arabs cover up for their family members—because of the far-reaching effects that can ruin someone later on. (This, incidentally, explains why "car accidents" account for so many deaths. No one to blame but fate…). So, adding the Arabic spin would make it the "Her *family* isn't good enough for my son—and our family" mentality.

In terms of occupation, every Arab parent pushes his or her child into the best field because they, the parents (and family!) ultimately take credit for the success (or failure!) of their children. For example, a girl who's fond of drawing might be forced into a career in medicine, since art isn't seen as a very respectable profession in the Arabic-speaking world; although this *is* beginning to change. If she sticks with oil-painting or hazmat-woodwork eco-statues (or selects a Ph.D. rather than an M.D.), she will forever be subjected to "WHY did Nermine Wagdi's *sorry* children end up as doctors? *What* did Nermine do that I didn't? **WHY GOD?!**"

Leading up to this push for top-level jobs, school-aged children are subjected to an interrogation at the end of each school day. The high points of this are:

1. Did you have a test today?

2. Did anyone get a higher grade?

3. Did you raise your hand in class?

4. Did the professor praise you in any way?

These topics obviously carry much significance, since the academic success that Junior attains reflects on the family. It's also the way to secure entry into the toughest programs in the best schools.

I remember an anecdote that I heard many years ago, at an Arab American conference. The speaker was a psychiatrist who frequently dealt with acculturation issues. He told of a young boy who had begun his junior-high career with full marks in every subject, until the fateful day that he discovered video games. His grades slipped lower and lower, until he had little better than a C average. At any rate, his mother confiscated the game, and his grades crept up again. One day, he made a 92 (the minimum required for an A). "Is that all?" his mother would ask. The next week, the grade had crept up to a 98. "Couldn't you have gotten a 100?" she asked, shaking her head and walking off. Finally, the boy had gotten what his mother had wanted, the 100. He smiled broadly, ready to accept a kiss and perhaps his video game. "A full mark, eh?" she asked. He nodded happily, beaming. In a voice of deceptive softness, she asked "Did anyone else get a 100?"

The boy looked confused. "Well, yes," he began. Mommy Dearest pressed her lips thinly together and muttered "*Ya khibti!*" ("oh, my failure!") before storming off.

Another aspect of collectivism that Westerners may find odd is the fact that unmarried children live with their parents, even if the "children" aren't children anymore. Despite the fact that this is beginning to change in the Middle East (and in the States, unfortunately), and even among Arab Americans, the rich Arab father has a responsibility to support his unmarried daughter until her marriage, which in some cases never happens (all bets are off if she's found a job, though). Arab American girls born to immigrant parents usually have to follow their father's rules, even if they don't live at home anymore (not saying they all do, though).

Yasmine, a 31-year-old Jordanian-American medical student, was cut off from all financial support once she was caught bringing a boyfriend to the apartment that her father had financed. I thought this was particularly sad, because her father had been a jolly man who loved his only daughter very much. He couldn't justify enabling his daughter to do things that he didn't approve of, however. Hence, the financial heave-ho.

Raising Children

As we've discussed, the institution of family dictates what one can and cannot do, based on what is good for the entire family and their honor. Accusations of not having being raised well make wonderful insults, such as "*ya aleel il adab!*" and "*ya mish mitrabi!*" both of which approximate "Oh, you with no upbringing!" To this end, fathers in Arab families are either dictators, browbeating their children into discipline, or big softies who charm their children into submission, but oftentimes both.

Unfortunately, the attempted discipline isn't attempted until the child is old enough to have already formed a personality, which is why Arab children are, more often than not, spoiled. On one hand, the spoiling doesn't really hurt too much—okay, so the kid might end up being a bit childish for the rest of his or her life, but no biggie. Having a close family that shows affection is worth it. But on the other hand, this childishness can be extremely irritating, and the cute "Opps, I didn't know I was overdrawn again!" obliviousness that was cute when Junior was a teenager isn't so cute once he's a married thirty-something throwing money away on beastly $1,000 shirts.

Mothers usually dote on their sons, to the point that some can wreak major havoc on their son's marriages. By the same token, Arab fathers often think that their daughters can do no wrong. For this reason, any falls from grace are that much more painful to them. Hence, the parents' ruthlessness in correcting (or punishing) their once-beloved.

Friendships

Arabs are very social beings, and their friendships run deep. A friendship can even begin from the first meeting, complete with arguments, confidences and favors.

I can remember when I moved into my first apartment. I was putting things away and sniffling, because my parents had just left and gone back to the home I'd grown up in. Suddenly, I heard a loud knock on the door. I froze, unsure of what to do. I *wanted* to open the door on the off-chance that my parents were still there, but I knew they couldn't be. My face was swollen with the tears of an entire day, so I knew that my visitor ran the risk of being turned into stone. I held my breath.

Just when I thought the visitor had gone, another knock sounded, louder than the first. I was beginning to feel like a character in an Edgar Allan Poe tale, when more pounding came, followed by my name in Arabic. I figured that an Arab couldn't be all that bad, and opened up. There stood an entire family! Youssef, his wife Maha, and their baby. They introduced themselves, and I informed them that my parents had just gone. Maha ran her eyes over my tear-stained face and playfully said that she had guessed that. We spoke for maybe five minutes that day, and I figured I wouldn't see too much more of them. But I was wrong. Not a week later, Maha had become my new best friend, and we chatted for hours every day. So now, years after that "chance" meeting, the three of them consider me family (and vice versa).

As previously mentioned, Arabs are social beings. So it's no surprise to learn how much Arabs love to talk! A chance meeting in a store or on the street can end up lasting half an hour or more. In-house visits can last until the wee hours of the morning. This is partly a result of the topics that Arabs love to discuss. At the top of the list are the West, religion, politics, other Arabic dialects, and attempts to marry off any unmarried people both parties are friendly with. Other popular topics are jobs, music and the concerns of daily life.

Hospitality

Hospitality is a huge deal in the Arab world. If someone is inhospitable, they're seen as cheapskates, yes, but they're also seen as the lowest form of human. For this reason, Arabs overcorrect in the form of "*ozooma*," or "the invitation." This involves (usually lovingly—*usually*) nagging the guest to eat, eat, eat! or drink something or even stay overnight.

This is not to imply that Arabs are only hospitable to avoid looking cheap—not by a long shot. Generosity is actually a command from the Koran, which we've already agreed has greatly influenced Arabic culture. (The Bible also teaches generosity, although Arab culture doesn't draw from Christianity). I once witnessed a girl complimenting an Egyptian friend's bracelet. The friend said "*itfadali!*" ("you're welcome to it!" or "go ahead!") and pushed it into the embarrassed girl's hand. The girl kept refusing, but the woman insisted, and the girl got to wear the 18k creation for almost a week before forcing the bracelet's owner to take it back.

Other forms of the Arabic hospitality include holding dinner until every last person is present, and sending food home with the guest. A hilarious example of this occurred not one month ago, when I was invited to a dinner party at the house of my friends Dr. Samy and his wife Magda. John, another friend from church, was invited, and so was his cousin. The actual tale begins a week beforehand, when I informed Magda that I was on a diet and could therefore not eat very much. At first, *she* informed me that I *was*, like it or not—but then she changed tactics and went along with me.

The evening itself started out with my late arrival (I had gotten lost). I was tardy by over two hours, and yet they had refrained from eating, even though I called at the one-hour mark and told them to eat up. At any rate, Magda handed me a plate and told me to fill it up. I chose heaping portions of *béchamel* and grape leaves, my favorites, to stave off goulash and other dishes that weren't at the top of my list. Every five minutes, my lovely hostess said "Sally! *Yalla!* You haven't eaten anything!" and I would dutifully take a small bite of something.

The gentlemen regaled me with tales of the Crusades that I'd never heard before, and I was so enthralled that I didn't even realize that Magda had made up a platter—not plate, but *platter*—of leftovers for me to take home. The amusing part is that we weren't halfway through dinner when she set it down on a table by the door. "*Hatakhdiiha!*" she crowed. ("You're taking it!"). My eyes glazed over and I knew that I couldn't refuse grape leaves, so my protests weren't even half-hearted, although I burst into laughter when I saw *two* platters that she sent home with John and his cousin.

In addition to sending food home, the Arab might blindly shake his or her head to one's pleas of "No! But I'm not going to eat it! It'll be a waste!" saying "*Walla yi himmini—ana aamalt illi aalaya!*" ("It doesn't matter to me! I did my part!").

Lateness

Anyone who's ever done any reading about Edward Hall's mono—and poly-chronic time model will understand that it's more a cultural thing (I think that Egyptians actually originated it) than a "my time is more important than yours" thing. If a Westerner (or Westernized Arab, most of whom don't have this problem) were to take offense at an Arab's (recurrent) lateness, he or she would be in error. This may sound very imperious, but there's literally no way to change the late-comer (as all of my friends and most of my ex-professors will tell you). Preparing everything the night before won't make a difference, and neither will waking up extra early. The "flaw" is in thinking one can achieve more than he or she usually could in the same amount of time, or else thinking one has extra time, leading to industrious tasks which require fixing (this always happens when I'm running ahead of schedule and decide that an extra dose of eyeliner never hurt anyone, after which I *always* botch it, after which I'm most likely heavy-handed with the makeup remover, after which I—tragically—end up with red eyes and a makeup job that went AWOL). That said, I'm now confident that it's universally understood why Arabs are always late (although I've merely explained the female side of things—I'm afraid to even venture a guess as to what *men* could find to keep themselves busy with while the clock keeps ticking away—mowing the lawn? Making a double-decker sandwich?).

Pleas and Excuses

Arabs tend to tell the WHOLE story behind a plea for something or an excuse. This comes from the fact that, in the Arabic-speaking world, one can always appeal to a higher power, such as one's boss at work, or a notary public who's just shut the office down for the day. (If the story isn't good enough, however, some Arabs turn to bribery). This is not to say that they are lying, because they usually aren't. They just happen to give about 400 percent more info than a Western audience is interested in hearing.

To illustrate this, here's what happens every time my friend Zahra (an immigrant Egyptian-American) pulls into the customer service desk at Wal-Mart:

Wal-Mart: Hi, d'you have a return?

Zahra: I brought you this lamp to return. It's so funny, because—

Wal-Mart: Is anything wrong with it, ma'am?

Zahra: Well, this is what happened—

Wal-Mart: Do you have the receipt ma'am?

Zahra: Well, that's what I was telling you, it's so funny because I originally bought this lamp because I needed one for my living room, but you see how the light bulb—

Wal-Mart: Oh, right. Uh, the receipt…?

Zahra: I thought you don't need a receipt? This is Wal-Mart! And anyway, I thought that since this lamp was made in the good old U.S.A.—

Wal-Mart: So you don't have the receipt? It's ok, ma'am. I'll just have to issue you—

Zahra: Wait! Put that gift card away! I have the receipt. It's right here. Do you see?

Wal-Mart: (presses lips together and fights to keep from rolling her eyes.) Yes, ma'am, I see it.

Zahra: The funny thing is that I bought it for my living room, but then my brother needed it in the guest room when he came to stay with us.

Wal-Mart: Alrighty, ma'am, that's a refund of $37.98. Thank you and have a nice day.

Zahra: So then, after we set up this lamp, the baby knocked it over and it broke the TV that I brought to you yesterday, I'm sure you remember? I was wearing the beige dress and—

Wal-Mart: I certainly *do* remember, ma'am…NEXT!

Crossing the Line

Some actions can be judged as having crossed the line, however. Obviously, different countries and even regions of the same country can have widely varying customs of greeting, even more so after religion gets thrown into the mix. The most common greeting is the handshake, which is acceptable in many regions and situations, although if both parties are the same gender, one follows the handshake with a kiss on each side of the face (let's call this the "Arab Greeting"). Yes, even the men!

Some Arab men don't touch women, even in a handshake, while others routinely give them a toned down version of the Arab Greeting I just mentioned, and yet *another* segment of the population tailors their contact to their feelings.

I once worked with a Saudi guy who shook my hand after clocking in every day, until one day, when he stopped. Puzzled, I asked if he had a cold. With typical Arab charm, he answered that he now suffered from another ailment which prevented him from shaking my hand again. I was confused until his brother, who also worked there, winked at me and gave a huge smile.

Some Moslem men place a handkerchief in their hand before shaking any non-Moslem's hand, while others don't. Age is another factor that guides who can greet whom—and in what manner.

For example, while it might be okay to give the college-aged son of my best friend a hug or the Arab Greeting, it wouldn't be appropriate for me to plant one on anyone I could conceivably marry—from a twentysomething cousin to a 40ish friend of the family who was widowed last year. It wouldn't even be that appropriate to hug a married man, actually, although Western customs have begun to seep into some parts of the Middle East (in fact, I'm sure that half of what I've just said may be seen as outdated by many, though not my parents). In other places, such as some regions of the Saiid in Egypt, a man and woman aren't even allowed to shake hands. (I don't—and never have—lived in the Saiid, and yet my parents would even frown upon a photo depicting me standing yards apart from a guy who doesn't share my last name. So much for old habits dying hard!).

Section 2: Hurdles—You Have to Understand *This* Stuff Before You Can Get Anywhere.

4

Bizarre Love Triangle—The Middle East, America and the West

Obstacles to a hassle-free acclimation into America include a love-hate relationship between the cultures involved. Exploring this, we ask—

- *Why does the Middle East seem to hate The West—and especially America?*
- *Why is the Middle East obsessed with America?*
- *How does America view the Middle East?*

All the Happiness That Money Can't Buy, and Other Lifestyle Issues

Well, maybe *hate* is a strong word. Middle East expert Daniel Pipes, in a recent article, suggested that "a country that is truly hated would not be under siege from illegal immigration, its popular culture would not dominate, and its model of government and economy increasingly emulated," thus implying that America is *resented*, rather than hated.

I agree and disagree, because on one hand (a very Western-sounding hand, I might add), he is correct about the immigration, culture and government—who in the world doesn't envy the success of this nation (a little superiority complex, hmm?)? At the same time, Pipes is speaking to concerns that are less Middle Eastern than global. Okay, so maybe Russia or Spain or England might emulate the United States, maybe people *do* try to sneak into the U.S., but many of those people would be happy to live here under almost any circumstances and probably only resent America because they're not on the winning team's side—for now.

I highly doubt that the people who actually *do* hate America (many sources tell me that it's actually the stricter Moslems who hate America), or at least hate its culture (a.k.a. "The Great Satan"), would want to live here, because what they object to most is what they would eventually drown in once they got here.

But, for the sake of argument, let's pretend that resentment *is* a factor, and see if we can't come up with some jealousy-makers—like the fact that not *only* do Mr. and Mrs. Joe Schmoe American have everything they want, (or so the world thinks) but if not, they can get it. In America, credit cards rule. So do financing, loans, leases and a hundred other variations on the basic "no money down" premise. Many nations don't have this, and neither do a number of Arab countries—and so there you have it—a feeling of "why can't *I* do that, too?"

Obviously, this feeling extends to many of the other forbidden fruits that Easterners have only dreamed about—like freedom, plenty, and consequence-free "romantic" relationships.

This is not to say that Americans don't have standards of their own, because they do. It's also not to hint that every single American in the whole planet lives in such a way, because every single American *doesn't*. It is to say, however, that, on the whole, "The East" holds her denizens to more restrictions than "The West"—and the Easterners are getting restless. (Some of them, anyway.)

Slightly more valid for our purposes is a *disdain for tradition and conventionality*. This dramatic phrase points to the fact that foreigners—but especially Arabs—have a feeling that America is a superpower that runs by the Almighty Dollar, not art, feelings, religion, etc. Arabs, among others, also sometimes feel as though Americans have "no heart," as demonstrated by their blatant individualism, capitalism, consumerism and materialism, but I, having grown up in the States, have met countless individuals who (in my mind) nullify this argument, but let's stay focused for now.

Another factor of Arabs' dislike of America could be the oft-hinted *permissiveness*, which I would actually list as a subset of the previous reason. This permissiveness doesn't only allude to one-night stands and wearing getups that show more skin than cover, although traditional Easterners frown upon both.

No—permissiveness is shown when 19-year-old Samir stays out all day without calling his mother to tell her that he's alive (and she allows it), when 22-year-old Magda insists on living alone when her parents live in the same town—it's the "do what you want without regard for your family" mentality. And since the Middle East is a collectivist culture, the considering of one's own needs or wants ("what's best for *me*") before his or her family's is not only the action of a selfish person (where selfish means "thinking of one's self"—the whole "I need to do this for me" or "I need to find out who *I* am" thing), but the action of a stranger.

One of the more memorable times that I came across this was when a kind (and somewhat bewildered) 40-something Egyptian immigrant I'd met a few times regaled me with an anecdote that I found more sad than anything else:

"I was on the phone with my daughter tonight, and she told me about a new Jordanian family that joined her church, about a great jacket she'd found on sale, about her promotion at work. We chatted for a bit longer, but it must have become increasingly obvious to her that I disapproved of certain things she was mentioning—her midnight trips to the supermarket, her refusal to come home for the holidays (heaven forbid that she might miss out on an evening out with the girls!), and the like. When I offered her some suggestions, she snapped at me, making accusations that I didn't respect her. Stunned, I replied that she was shutting me out of her life, treating me like a stranger. She became very quiet for a moment, before telling me that if being treated as a stranger was the only way to get some respect around the family, then so be it. Needless to say, the conversation didn't last too much longer." The woman didn't say too much more, but I had the distinct impression that she regretted having brought her children up in America, rather than Cairo.

For the record, this same Prodigal Daughter chose her best friend's rehearsal dinner over her brother's doctoral graduation ceremony. His take? He was more annoyed that she didn't show any desire to have attended it, and that she showed no sorrow for having missed it. "Graduations happen all the time and they're no big thing," he told me, two years after the fracas. "But she's shown her true colors, now. Now I know that I should never rely on her again. She's not related to me. If she needs me, I'm there for her—that's what family's for, though the fact seems to have slipped her mind. But our friendship—gone."

Next we find the relative *immorality* of the Western world, although the term *immoral* could be seen as ethnocentric in favor of the East, since that's the way Easterners are *supposed* to be, and anything apart from *that* is "immoral." Conversely, calling the East "uptight" or "repressed" or "strict" would be Euro-or Americentric, but since we're looking at it through the lens of the Arab world, we'll stick to the former.

In America, a 28-year-old unmarried woman would not only be *allowed* to have a casual relationship with a man, she might be pushed into it by well-meaning friends (or family!) who fear that she "doesn't get out enough" or "works too hard." In films like "The Wedding Singer" and "Swingers," the trusty sidekicks have no higher wish than finding their chums a companion for a no-strings-attached night of fun. In almost every romance novel ever penned, the rich, muscular hero shows more than a bit of dismay upon finding himself in love with a...gulp...*virgin*.

Ok, so maybe these examples were biased, having been chosen from the media and not real life. But. The fact that these examples can be gotten away with, the fact that an American man could *consider* a woman his friend used to date, or one whom he noticed on the arm of another man—impossible in the Middle East. The fact that an American woman could consent to cohabit with a man she's not married to—impossible. The fact that an engaged couple in America can go away for a weekend together without raising eyebrows (or calling in the religious police)—well, I'll spare you this last melodramatic "*impossible!*"

By the way, as we all know by now, Arabic culture takes many things from Islam, meaning that many Christian Arabs feel the same way about relative immorality, et al., though Western attitudes are creeping in and taking hold in Christian and Moslem pockets of the Middle East alike (apparently, modernization = Westernization). Despite their feeling that The West is a haven of immorality, some radical Islamic groups are actually anti-American by virtue of the fact that America is allegedly a "Christian nation," although one can't really call it that anymore—it's become "the land of religious freedom," though some might argue with *this*, in the light of such recent rulings as the removal of the Ten Commandments from an Alabama courthouse, and also from a Montana courthouse lawn (said people might take issue with the fact that *any* religious statues were removed, since freedom would allow *all* religions to thrive, and post their beliefs for all to see, if they wanted. On the other hand, keeping the monuments may have signified that the government was endorsing Christianity, but enough of that).

The Past

One editor of a University of North Carolina, Chapel Hill newsletter cites a lingering bitterness over colonialism as the reason for the Middle East's dislike of the West: "*Beginning with Napoleon at the close of the eighteenth century, French, British, and Italian incursions carved up the Ottoman Empire to the extent that nearly all North African and Middle Eastern 'countries' were held in colonial thrall until the second half of the twentieth century.*"

That's lovely, but there are a few reasons why I would set this reason near the bottom of the list: For one, I highly doubt that the *entire* Middle East is fully educated in *all* of the historical and governmental goings-on that have occurred in the past three or so centuries, and carry this grudge about, *and* hate the West solely for this reason, (by the same token, ask yourself how many Americans can find Maine, Oklahoma and Indiana on the map. Yeah, that's what I thought.) although if one revisits the "radical Islamists against Christian nations" argument, one would stumble upon The Crusades as yet another strike against the nation whose alleged religion carried it out (although proponents of the Crusades maintain that they didn't go looking for trouble and gratuitous bloodshed—they just wanted to prevent their beloved religion, Christianity, from being stamped out by the Arab invaders—at first, anyway).

On the other hand, many Black Americans keep bringing up slavery, Native Americans haven't forgotten about their veritable ousting, and many Jews (American and not) remember the whole Moses thing and mention anti-Egyptian feelings consistently. Even though maybe—*maybe*—one percent of the (still living) members of these three groups have actually *gone* through any of these injustices first-hand, the other 99 percent may still be living with the consequences of these happenings. They may have felt bitterness since the day they learned to walk, but they weren't there to witness the events that would ultimately cause their ill feelings towards others.

U.S. Policy and other Machinations

At the top of the list of "Why?" is the U.S. policy towards the Palestinians and Israel, especially America's blind support of the latter. ABC News' Chris Bury and Richard Gizbert quote Palestinian-American Michael Terazzi in a September 2003 report:

"It's not lost on any Palestinian that the bombs that are dropping are dropped by American-made F-16s, by American-made Apache helicopters. The tear gas that's fired at us is American-made, the bullets that are shot at us are American-made…It's not lost on the average Palestinian that it's American economic support, financial support, military support and political support that, in effect, denies us our freedom."

But there's more. America's un-evenhanded rulings, as well as the oppression of the Iraqis during the early '90s (and again at the start of this Millennium) serve only to heighten discord between the States and the Middle East. Add to that the strength and almost-constant presence of U.S. troops and you've got a veritable re-creation of the Western colonial occupation of the Middle East.

Keep in mind that the Arab world has enough internal conflicts, restrictions and repressions on their own without the West's snooping into their affairs—is it any wonder that many Arabs are less than fond of the U.S.?

In a hard-hitting January 2003 article, The Middle East Media Research Institute (MEMRI) postulates that America, acting as nothing more than a lackey to the Zionist Lobby, is a vampire itching to sink its teeth into oil-rich Saudi Arabia. The piece goes on to suggest that America is "helping" the Middle East by teaching it democracy "in the service of American interests," with the added "bonus" of replacing Arab society with one not unlike America's (*yadel moseeba!*). Khaled Al-Suleiman, author of an article titled "My Advice To You, Mr. Powell" put it this way:

> What…Powell means by his plan to turn us into a modern society is not that every Saudi will become a computer engineer or…researcher, but that we will be freed from what he considers the moral bonds of our social behavior. He wants us to become a modern society, like his…in which fathers are stripped of the freedom to raise their children…in which the marriage of minors is a crime, but sexual relations with minors is permitted!! He means a society stripped of its identity…values, and virtues—an ugly society with no connection to its roots.

Al-Suleiman goes on to challenge politicians to *"devote a little time every day to sitting in front of the television and watching the famous American talk shows whose programs are broadcast unceasingly, so that you will learn how lucky we are to lag behind your caravan of modernity."*

So, while it's nice of America to want to bring the Middle East "up to speed," many Arabs can't see any advantage to it. As Patrick Buchanan put it, *"If Islamic peoples detest America, why not let them discover democracy in their own time, rather than trying to convert them with thermobaric bombs and cruise missiles?"*

Politics Aside…

On the subject of "lagging behind," there are many Arab practices (Islamic and not) which, to the West, paint the Middle East as needing to be "rescued" and dragged into the 21st century. We've already covered the official stuff, about oil and democracy and other solely political issues, but there are other issues that deserve mention, including women and freedom.

In terms of women's alleged imprisonment and restriction, I have found literally dozens of Arab sources, both in books and in person, who have scoffed at this, including a great many Moslem women who are grateful for the *higab*, commenting that they don't get harassed, attacked, or otherwise bothered while clad in the modest garment. These same women and others go on to mention that they find it amusing that the world, meaning the West, feels sorry for them and their "plight," ignoring the fact that they, in many cases, chose to put on the veil, or to stay in an "oppressive" environment when they could have "escaped" to a more permissive society. Some of the women, however, take this "sympathy" as more of a condescending attitude (maybe they consider it to be the social equivalent of U.S. policy?).

In terms of freedom, a majority of my Arabic-speaking interviewees (especially those with children), both Christian and Moslem, residents of either America or their native lands, have said that they preferred their more restricted society to the American, because at least back home, they didn't have the freedom to even *try* something that could prove harmful to their reputation, health, or spiritual life; while the strict Middle Eastern culture is beginning to Westernize, there is still a much smaller incidence of Arab teenagers having tried drugs or having engaged in illicit sexual contact (where illicit means extramarital) than in America. Does that mean that Arabs only refrain from such behavior as a result of the strenuous external controls present? Or perhaps the huge role that religion plays in the Middle East has made it easier to abstain? Either way, the result is the same.

At the same time, however, many of these same people have expressed gratefulness for the very same freedoms that they were denied back home. Taking this to the extreme, we stumble upon a small (but growing) segment of the Arabic-speaking population, which includes those who behave like *Nofal*, the on-screen cousin of Adel Imam's character in the excellent movie "Hello, America!" For those of you who haven't seen the film, I highly recommend it; for those of you who have, I'm sure the image of Nofal's wife, shedding tears over the fact that her 16-year-old daughter was still a virgin, is imprinted on your brain. To someone like me (who draws the good from both Western and Arabic cultures), it's a depressing image in general, but more so, because, as I said, life is imitating art (or is it the other way around?) and more and more people are beginning to behave the same way; that is, wanting to forget their culture, roots, language, etc.

One thing both conservative immigrants and Nofal-ites agree on, however, is that in America, there is less religious persecution (although it seems that some liberals want to end conservatism—once and for all—which isn't very liberal of them, but anyway), less governmental corruption (in terms of widespread bribery, anyway) and in general, fewer hassles (more on that later, though).

This brings us to another point, another query situated at the other end of the spectrum:

Why Is the Middle East Obsessed With America?

Whether staying back home or actually moving to America, Arabs can't seem to get enough of it (despite everything I just told you in the last section). There are a number of widely cited reasons for both the mass immigrations of the First and Second Waves (1875-1925, and 1945 and after, respectively), and the tendency to do something "because Americans do it," which Arabs have dubbed "*Okdat il Khawaga*" or "the Foreign Complex" (which my mother ordered me to tell you does *not* affect all Arabs). But let's start at the very beginning, a very good place to start.

Why the West?

Despite being guilty of the afore-mentioned "crimes" against Middle Easterners and their part of the world, the West—but especially America—remains the example for many aspects of Arab life. As with everything to do with the Middle East, there are greatly differing points of view regarding this, but that's only to be expected in a region of the world that's home to so many dialects, denominations and interests.

On the one hand, as we've covered (ad nauseum), most Arabs would rather die than give up their culture, but on the other hand, almost everything they do these days bears the fingerprint of the West: Egyptians drink Pepsi and Starbucks, Saudis drive Volvos, and many Middle Eastern countries have shows that rival *Good Morning, America*, down to the miniskirts and blonde highlights in the anchorwoman's hair. It's important to remember, of course, that this Westernization is more acceptable now than it was in earlier years, so an Arab who became an American citizen in the '60s or '70s might be more than a bit surprised to note that teenagers back home may stay out late and have friends of the opposite sex nowadays. A distant cousin of mine (American for 20 years) was still astounded—months after the fact—that during her first winter pilgrimage to Egypt in about 17 years, a friend attending the same Christmas party pressed a glass of Jack Daniels into her hand. "I don't understand," began my cousin, obviously on top of her game that day. "It's whiskey," she was told haughtily. "Yes, but why?" she asked. The friend shot her a disbelieving glance. "To celebrate! We're just like you, now. We drink liquor and do all of the things that Americans do! Drink up!" My cousin didn't even bother to hide her rolling eyes.

Why Do They Come?

While there are a number of reasons that any given Arab might give for emigration, these are the most widely held: *Financial opportunity* (a greater number of people can actually LIVE here, and prosper), *prosperity* (there's a wider range of available luxuries here), the aforementioned "*Okdat il Khawaga*" (wowsers, light hair and blue eyes!), also known as the "Grass Is Greener" syndrome, and finally *freedom*, in its many forms.

In terms of finances, we've already agreed that the rampant loans and credit cards in America can make life go by more smoothly, although anyone will tell you that racking up debt wreaks jaggedness rather than smoothness. I know a fair number of recently naturalized Arabs who have fallen in love with credit and into its trap, although I know an equal number who aren't used to them and thus use their credit cards to buy things they can afford, paying the entire balance every month.

Another aspect of financial life is the job market. In America, jobs carry benefits and other compensations that some Arab countries don't have. In addition, there is more money to be had, as well as more opportunity for above-average income and entrepreneurship. Most Middle Eastern countries have a per capita Gross Domestic Product ranging between $500 and $5,000 U.S. per year, though the numbers for such places as Qatar and the Emirates are over $20,000 (CIA Factbook, 2003)—is it any wonder, then, that members of the hard-working Arab nations welcome the chance to come and be rewarded for their efforts?

In terms of prosperity, America is, without question, one of the most prosperous nations in current history; there are many things available here not easily available in other lands, and more of them available should one want them. It's not uncommon to have three cars and eight TVs in America. It's not unheard of to eat dinner in a restaurant five times (or more) a week. It's hardly rare to have a den, parlor, formal dining room and breakfast room in the same house. For the right price, one can get almost anything in America.

Okdat il Khawaga is the name used to refer to Arabs' fascination with all things foreign, but focusing mostly on the Western (Americans also suffer from this, only *they* think that anything out of Europe is automatically great, and any clothing to bear an Italian label is worth obscene amounts of cash. Or credit, as the case may be).

Because of this, some Arabs speak with the most elementary level of Arabic they can muster (keep in mind that this is their first language), so as to appear foreign or well traveled (this is half the reason why Egyptians coo over me when I go back for visits). Unfortunately, many Arab Americans' Arabic dulls (naturally) over the years, until they sound more like foreigners than Arabs. Other times, they apply their new accent to their old language, resulting in the especially amusing "Manhattan Palestinian Dialect" and the especially horrifying "Chipola Springs Maghrebi Dialect."

Okdat il Khawaga is also the motivating force behind many actions of Arabs and recent immigrants, including drinking alcohol (when they've spent their entire lives as teetotalers), looking down upon the use of Arabic or the enjoyment of any Arabic media, such as songs, films, plays and the like, or even dressing in shorts and/or miniskirts at all times (since they're frowned upon in much of the Middle East). Obviously, being in a land that not only allows but sometimes encourages these behaviors is more than enough to get the new immigrants on their way to stocking their new dens with Jack Daniels, or replacing their Adel Imam film collection with Billy Crystal's greatest hits.

And in terms of appearance? Forget about it—in America, they're surrounded with their ideal of beauty. Yes, *Okdat il Khawaga* is what's responsible for the widespread fixation on the aforementioned light hair and eyes, extending to the paleness of skin (which is the other half of why Egyptians love me—I'm quite pale, more than I'd like. Having been brought up in the States, of course, *I'm* somewhat obsessed with getting a tan. Hah! What was I saying about the grass being greener?).

In terms of our last reason, religious freedom probably tops the list. There are a number of reasons for this. Let's examine it from the Moslem perspective first: Islam is the most widespread religion in the Middle East, creating too strict of a life for nominal Moslems. This isn't just because the neighbors can see everything from their kitchen window, but because many things just aren't available in the Arab world. For the guy who wants a girlfriend for the weekend or a fifth of vodka, the Middle East is no place to be. So, he moves here.

Now, the Christian perspective. While I can't make a blanket statement for all of the Christians in the Middle East, I believe I can get away with saying that life there is rough for pretty much everyone (meaning all religions and races), but especially Christians. This is not to say that people go out of their way to harass Christians, (though some people do) but that the life there is set up for the existence of Moslems, and Christians just don't fit in anymore. It's kind of like being a Russian in a town that only speaks French; No one is *squelching* the Russian language, it's just that things happen to cater to those who speak French.

Of course, there are those, such as authors Daniel Pipes and Joseph Farah, who would say that Christians are *very* persecuted in the Middle East, citing that if things don't change, the population of 12 million Christians living in Arab countries will be cut in half by 2020. There are also those who mention the thousands of slaughtered Assyrians, as in this snippet from the website for the State of Assyria:

> From 1900 to 1945, the Turks, Kurds, Arabs and Persians committed genocides against the Assyrian people and on all other Christian peoples in Asia Minor [Middle East]. These international human rights violations were crimes against humanity and served as examples for future atrocities of this manner in Europe. In these genocides, 750,000 indigenous Christian Assyrians of Turkey, Syria, Iraq, and Iran, including millions of Christian Armenians and Greeks were burned, slaughtered, and shot indiscriminately and systematically. Defenseless men, women, children and the elderly all became victims of these inconceivable brutalities. (Atour, 2003)

In addition to these tragedies is a more recent one—the modern movement to quell the Aramaic language (maybe to force the Assyrians into becoming "mainstream Arabs?")

There are *also* those who would mention the 1200 Copts who have been killed in Egypt during the past ten years. Reports such as the following aren't uncommon in Upper Egypt:

"On December 31, 1999…Moslems rioted, attacked and killed 21 Christians in the village of Al-Kosheh, southern Egypt."

"Gunmen believed to be Islamic militants, wielding assault rifles and wearing masks and military fatigues, walked into this predominantly Christian hamlet 300 miles south of Cairo around 6:30 p.m. and shot everyone in sight."

In addition to this blatant persecution is the fact that it's illegal for Copts to rebuild their fallen churches. Changing this law is only one of twenty requests that Copts have put together, found at copts.net. Here are the most interesting other ones (to me, anyway):

> *"After centuries of discrimination and intermittent persecution, the Christians of Egypt demand that they be treated equally. At the turn of the 21st century, in a world in which human freedoms are considered innate and*

inalienable rights, Egypt's Copts still face inequitable treatment within their own homeland.

1. Copts want all Egyptian citizens to enjoy religious freedoms, including the freedom to change one's religion. All individuals, regardless of religion, must enjoy the right to convert to the faith of their choice, without fear of imprisonment, torture, or any and all forms of harassment.

2. Copts want a serious and determined effort by the Egyptian government to apprehend those who perpetrate violence against Christians. Aggressors must be punished to the fullest extent of the law, and victims must be adequately compensated. To date, all those who have murdered Copts have received little or no punishment for their acts of violence, communicating to extremist groups and others that Copts may be murdered with impunity.

3. Copts want the 19th century Hamayouni decree abolished. This outmoded decree requires that the president of Egypt approve all permits for church construction. In contrast, mosques in Egypt are built with no such restrictions.

6. Copts want an end to the forced conversion of Christian girls, who are kidnapped and raped by Muslim extremist groups.

7. Copts want the religious affiliation record removed from national identification cards and employment applications so as to eliminate the facilitation of discriminatory practices against religious minorities."

A final reason for an Arab's exodus from his or her homeland is eviction, just as we've seen with the Copts and Assyrians, or as in the case of the Palestinians (Christians and Moslems alike) who have been driven from their homes.

Will the Aramaic language be saved? Will the Copt's demands be met? Who can tell, really? In the meantime, one can see why 77 percent of the Arabs in America are Christians.

5

How Does America (pre-and post-September 11ᵗʰ) View the Middle East?

Many Americans are less than fond of the Middle East. This could be because they don't understand our culture, and thus fear it. It could also be because they see Middle Easterners as "primitive" and "backwards," hiding their women away and living in caves that don't even have microwaves or Internet access.

The Western media's coverage of Arabs hasn't helped anything, either; in countless surveys, Americans have expressed the following stereotypes concerning Arabs: sheikhs, terrorists (or other villains), cabbies, owners of gas stations, "desert dwellers," belly dancers (the women, obviously, which is amusing, since Moslem women, a majority of Arab women, are veiled) or marauders. Film expert Jack Shaheen points out that children never get any Arab heroes to cheer for. For those who might mention the positive message found in Disney's *Aladdin*, may I remind you that the "positive" example was undermined by the fact that Aladdin was portrayed as a thief—albeit good-hearted. Sadly, many Americans feel that Arabs aren't capable of doing anything worth cheering for.

Americans and Their Society

American society is unique: it's allowed built-in obsolescence to push national sales into the trillions (skeptical, eh? Find *one* thing around your house that's seven years old, that people *still* use *and* still works). It's become the global poster child for George Ritzer's notion of McDonaldization (characterized by *efficiency, calculability, predictability, increased control,* and *the replacement of humans by non-human technology*). And it's promoted convenience and instant gratification in almost every sector. Don't believe me? Then don't freak out next time your 20-

minute oil change takes 35, don't whine about the extra day that the While-U-Wait cleaners are going to need to *fully* remove that gravy stain from your favorite suit, and for Pete's sake, stop rolling your eyes when you find out that the French fries you just ordered are going to take another three minutes to cook.

A clever program on PBS has added a new ailment to the roster of these American specialties—"Af-flu-en-za, n. 1. The bloated, sluggish and unfulfilled feeling that results from efforts to keep up with the Joneses. 2. An epidemic of stress, overwork, waste and indebtedness caused by dogged pursuit of the American Dream. 3. An unsustainable addiction to economic growth." But just what is it that Americans have been spending so much on? Cars? Trips? Electronics? Houses? All of the above, says CNNMONEY, in a 2003 report. But these ever-increasing economic and industrial trends are just a few of the hallmarks of American—and Western—culture.

Moving on to the interpersonal spectrum, we find many trends relating to Americans and the ways they interact, both with other Americans, and everyone else. According to Gary Althen, author of *American Ways—a Guide for Foreigners in the United States* (1988), Americans tend to live by the values of individualism, equality, informality, change, progress, efficiency, achievement, assertiveness and directness, generally looking towards the future and believing in a basic goodness of humanity. For example, a woman can get a hotel room without the necessity of a husband's or brother's presence, a homeless Pakistani-American has the same rights as a Jewish millionaire CEO, that same CEO (or the president of the U.S.) can be seen in sweaty workout clothes without creating a national scandal.

In Althen's words:

> Americans are trained to conceive of themselves as separate individuals, and…assume everyone else in the world is, too. When they encounter a person from abroad who seems to them excessively concerned with the opinions of parents, with following traditions, or with fulfilling obligations to others, they assume that the person feels trapped or is weak, indecisive…They assume, furthermore, that after living for a time in the United States people will come to feel liberated from the constraints arising outside themselves and will be grateful for the opportunity to "do their own thing" and "have it their own way."

Althen goes on to mention other phrases Americans tend to live by, such as "You'll have to decide that for yourself," "I need some time to myself," "age of independence," "Look out for number one," and "You made your own bed, now lie in it." Needless to say, these phrases are not part of Middle Eastern culture.

Nor, actually, the atmosphere in my own home (nor the homes of thousands of other first-generation Arab Americans).

Some examples drawn from my own life involve four of my dearest American friends: Josh is Jewish, American, and very liberal. He believes that I should do anything to better myself, even accepting that perfect job 3,000 miles and three time zones away from my family. Matthew is a second-generation Italian American who often tells me how silly I am for not going against the wishes of my parents and accepting dates (I live many hours from them and could, technically, get away with anything). Linda (dear, sweet Linda) is half Japanese and uber American, yet ultra cosmopolitan, as a result of her many years in the military. She thinks that I should just live my life the way I want to, whether that means dating, traveling 3,000 miles, or partying like a rock star. Finally, Lacy is a fine Southern woman who understands how important my family and traditions are to me. At the same time, however, she is the most self-reliant person I know, never asking for help from anyone and always there for others (read: me), advising on how disasters should be fixed, how things are supposed to be done, and *why*. The reason Lacy is included as an example here is because in past years, finding a Middle Eastern woman who knew as much as men did (if not more) about real life, problem solving and troubleshooting was somewhat rare (well, being allowed to *act* on it, anyway).

Another trait I've noticed in Americans (and many other Westerners) is their tolerance and even encouragement of fields that are considered iffy by Easterners. Like the time(s) when certain family members scoffed at my decision to pursue fine arts in college (I ended up switching to psychology, which still wasn't good enough). Like the time when these same family members intimated that my work as a photographer could only ever be a hobby, begging me to cease and find "a real job." Like the time when I ran into Dr. Roshan's widow.

Dr. Roshan had brought his wife and toddlers over from Calcutta in the late '70s, settling into the role of family friend soon after. Many years passed, and we lost touch with them, although there was the occasional sighting at the supermarket, accompanied by the predictable wave, air kiss, and promise to call. Rather recently, I was shopping for eye shadow with an American friend when I heard a familiar voice. "Sally!" caroled Mrs. Roshan, whom I hadn't seen in about three years. My face broke into a smile when I saw her, though the smile dropped when I noticed that she was dressed in black. She shook her head, sadly, and answered my question before I asked it. "Yes, my husband is dead. Cancer. Ah, well at least he's at rest now," she finished. I hugged her and offered my condolences, until she changed the subject to me and my latest news. I told her, then asked about her children. "Well," she began, "Nisha finally finished medical school and is now interning at University Hospital." I offered my congratulations and asked about the younger Roshan girl. Mrs. Roshan's eyes grew hard, and her voice took on a cooler tone than I had ever heard it take. "Meeta got into an Ivy League…she will begin work on her Ph.D. in the fall. Don't ask me what her major will be, because I can't bear the thought that it's…Journalism!!" My American friend, who had been silent throughout the exchange, said "Wow! That is sooooo cool!"

Mrs. Roshan cast a hunted look over her shoulder before rapping out, "She is going to an Ivy League—at no small cost to us, I might add—for *journalism*! What does she need a Ph.D. for in that field? More importantly, how can she waste time on such a field in the first place! I tell you…" Shaking her head in disgust, Mrs. Roshan patted me on the cheek and went to the housewares section, still muttering to herself. I hid a smile, though my friend looked baffled. "How can you smile when that poor lady just had a freak-out session in front of you?" she asked, making me seem as heartless as a bottle of water. I cast an amused glance over at her and shook my head. "She wasn't going crazy, she just hasn't changed in 25 years, that's all. Don't you know that there are only three great jobs in the Middle East? Physician/pharmacist, engineer/college professor and religious leader." "But India isn't in the Middle East," my friend objected. "Oh yeah. Well, you know how things are in the East, and an Easterner is an Easterner is an Easterner," I said, in a perfect example of the proper stereotype-free political correctness that Arabs are so famous for. Hah.

Speaking of stereotypes and other feats of prejudicial behavior, Americans, though outwardly against it, tend to make assumptions about people in front of them, even if they don't actually discriminate. I was reminded of this when I and some Arab friends, including my friend Sam (a filmmaker) recently attended an area film festival that featured his work. One of the last films in the first half of the evening featured lots of action and lovely remixes of songs by Egyptians Amr Diab and Ehab Tawfiq, and Lebanese sensation Haifa Wahby. During the intermission, I and my very Arabic looking and sounding friends were accosted by a man who was impressed with the film. "You did an excellent job! You should really be proud of your work!" We all exchanged glances, brows lifted and puzzlement in our eyes. "The film with the kickboxer, right?" said the man, slowly, as though we couldn't understand him—or his language. Sam's expression got a bit frosty, but he managed a smile as he replied. "Actually, they haven't played my film yet."

Anti-foreigner? Moi?

I've always detected a hint of anti-foreigner sentiment in America; "Look at all these dang foreigners taking up all the housing and jobs!" I've heard.

What these people don't realize is that most of these foreigners, many of whom are naturalized, and thus *not* foreign, or else born here with a different set of features or skin tone, either do work that no one else will do, or bring their experience and expertise over, improving America and lengthening her roster of achievements in many different fields.

Anti-foreign and anti-Arab sentiment has grown in the U.S., though, for a very different reason (but more on that—and the now-infamous September 11, in chapter 13)...

Section 3:
Roadblocks—The Issues
Faced by Arab Americans

o o o o o o o o o o o o o o o o o o o o o o o o o o o o o o o o o

"Roses have thorns and shining waters mud…
And cancer lurks deep in the sweetest bud…
Clouds and eclipses stain the moon and the sun…
And history reeks of the wrongs we have done…"

—Gordon Sumner

6

Courtship, Marriage and the Ubiquitous "Dating Thing"

Pick a song, any song, the ones from the top. That's right, think of any American Top 40 tune and consider the lovey-dovey words, the "I can't live without you!" words, the "let's dive into that broom closet and get to know each other" words. Maybe those are poetic in their *own* way, but, well…

Arabs, on the other hand—arguably the most romantically-minded people on the planet—have a knack for putting their feelings in more heartfelt terms than in the likes of such songs as "Hit Me, Baby, One More Time" (Britney's claim to fame) and N Sync's "I Want You Back." For example, Lebanese singer Asy el-Hellani sings "*Wi'n kan aalaya/addilak enayya/bass inta tirda/wi't'hissi bayyaa,*" which means "If it was up to me, I would give you my eyes, just so you would agree/accept and feel me/my presence." And Egyptian singer Amr Diab, in "Ayzeen Yighayarook," sings "*Yakhdo enaya, y'shofook,*" which translates into "If they took my eyes, they would see you (in them)." But relationships don't always start out that way…

For my fellow first-gens, get ready to hide a smirk, because your life story is likely hidden somewhere in this chapter. For the uninitiated—that is, the person who's never had a thing to do with the Arab way of doing things (namely dating)—I advise you to buckle up. You're going to hear some things in this chapter that'll make your teeth itch.

First Comes Marriage, Then the Baby Carriage, *Then* Love (if you're lucky).

Sometimes it happens like the movies—two people see one another across a crowded room, hearts connecting the same moment their eyes do. More often than not, however, the future spouses are the victims of matchmaking attempts or chance meetings at religious centers (though in some cases, a man will learn about someone's daughter or sister or friend—sight unseen—and then drop by her house for a visit with Daddy). More often than not, an arsenal of roguish tricks assists the potential lovebirds in securing affections and ascertaining feelings.

At any rate, under the old regime, the Arab man learns about a potential bride, asks about her, and then—as early as the same day, in some cases—enters into an engagement contract with her. In more Westernized Arab cities, however, fewer and fewer couples enter into an engagement so quickly, opting instead to learn more about one another before signing on the dotted line. Every region also has its own pattern of arranging things, and its own particular timetable for doing so. I think it's safe to say, however, that a good deal of Middle Easterners who still live there aren't "in love with" their intended when they say "I do"—at least not in the "Sleepless in Seattle"/"Wuthering Heights" sense. Many American women take a proposal as a sign that things are going great, and that an "I love you" is on the horizon. American men are generally quick to forgive the woman they love, because they would rather spend the rest of their lives *with* her than without. Arabs, on the other hand, are looking for a spouse who fits their criteria, and generally don't stick around too long if something unsavory appears out of their almost-spouse's past.

The biggest deal-breakers are dishonesty, having hidden something, and being damaged goods (these obviously overlap, in most cases), although, true to Middle Eastern form, a *man* would be forgiven most of these, while a woman would get dropped like nobody's business.

In terms of dishonesty, one may have lied about his or her age. I was especially sad to hear about a girl who had spent almost 15 months engaged to a man who loved her dearly. They were both professional, successful first-generation Americans; her family hailed from Port Saiid, while his family, who loved her as their own, came from Aswan. On one of her birthdays, his family threw a celebration, inviting all of the Egyptian families in the area. All was well until it was time to open the gifts; as her soon-to-be mother-in-law read card after card aloud (to the girl's delight), one card made Aunty stop in her tracks "To Rania, the sweetest and best girl, on your 27th birthday! God bless!"

His mother's face drained of color, but she pressed her lips into a tight smile that no one really picked up on. Making an excuse, she managed to sequester both families. "Is it true that your daughter is twenty-SEVEN?" she demanded. "Yes, but you've known this for over a year," answered the girl's father, suspecting his future sister-in-law of madness. "But my SON," she screeched, "is only twenty-FIVE!! You said she was *younger* than he was! *Khalas!*" It didn't matter to her that her son was almost 26, that he couldn't have cared less if his intended had been 30, or that the misinformation was actually due to a well-meaning relative of the groom's mother. Alas, what the mother said went, and there was more than a hint of sadness in his eyes as he turned to stare at her one last time.

Other than age, a girl can lie about having been engaged before, about her extent of sexual experience, or even about her opinions. Arabs obviously don't have a corner on the prospective bride's lying market, but in many cases, the deal's off once the falsehood is unearthed.

In terms of hiding things (close relative of "lying"), a girl might hide her previous involvement or even friendship with another man (some Arabs can be very suspicious of a mere friendship), any physical involvement with these same men, and illnesses in her family, either physical or emotional. If you'll remember, Arab families tend to steer clear of families with illnesses among their members because they feel that it will have affected the person, and also because of heredity, unlike many Americans, whose attitude when in love is more often than not "We'll get through this together! I'm here for you," rather than the Arab response of "um…see ya!" On the other hand, one Saiidi friend of mine alleges that it was her refusal of her previous fiancé's repeated attempts to seduce her that made her now-husband admire her and propose.

The third deal breaker, as I've mentioned, is the state of being "damaged goods." Many Arabic women I know disregarded the fact that their suitors were playboys prior to the engagement, declaring, "He picked *me*, though, didn't he?" Some men feel almost the same, citing "It's what happens *after* the marriage that counts!" For the woman to feel this way is almost expected (rather unreadily, sometimes), but it's something of a rarity for the man to feel this way. More common are the men who are out for blood, so to speak, but more on that later. For now, let's start in on the roguish tricks that I mentioned earlier…

Roguish Tricks

Most people will agree that love is a game. As previously mentioned, some of the male players take the bull by the horns and ask for an engagement immediately. Other players might send their mother over as an ambassador of goodwill, still others spend months engaged in a staring competition with their quarry, whether because they wish to know more about her, be more certain of their own feelings for her, or even because they really *are* too shy to say anything. Their shyness isn't of the "aww, shucks!" nature—rather, it's the sort that arises when the player isn't sure how his target will respond. After all, if she's a good and virtuous girl, the player should never even suspect her of having noticed him. But maybe I'm getting ahead of myself. Though this study in coyness, *the secret admirer*, as I've dubbed it, was more popular in past generations and larger (rather than smaller) gatherings, it can be found (to this day) wherever Arabs collect. Here's how it generally plays out: An Arab of the female persuasion ignores a man or frowns intensely at him, even behaving brusquely or impolitely towards him (if he happens to come near her). Any respectable Arab man will immediately know that not only is she interested, but respectable, since overt symbols are seen as signs of immorality. If the man is a non-Arab, however, he will think that she dislikes him or is not interested. Of course, this is named the *secret admirer* because the female's regard is supposed to be kept secret.

One famous trick used by suitors is the overt and artificially clumsy brush against the lady's arm or leg. If she smiles at him, she's seen as immoral (surprise, surprise). If she ignores him, she's thought to enjoy it (some would disagree with this assessment, however), but if she apologizes, she's seen as good and proper, and the courtship can go on to the next step, which is the curt nod.

In some parts of the Middle East, there are even prearranged non-verbal signals that mean different things—like the one wherein an unmarried man takes one sip from a full glass of water or lemonade, then hands it off to a girl. Many people would interpret this in different ways, such as "I guess *some*one bit off more than he could chew!" or "what a waste!" or even, "If I move now, *I* can be the first to snatch that glass away!" For a Nineties kind of girl hailing from parts of the Saiid, among others, it's taken as an overt invitation of courtship. So she should take care not to get *too* thirsty, or else find herself with an ardent suitor on her hands.

Of course, these tricks aren't the *only* ones available to a young person who wants to get married (the more resourceful Arabs devise methods as they go along). Furthermore, tricks can be used by anyone who fancies him or herself a matchmaker, especially siblings and mothers. For example, the married brother of a single young man who's *in absentia* might just deposit his two-year old into the arms of an unsuspecting beauty that he's noticed a few times. The toddler's mother appears from nowhere and magically snaps a photo, then sails over to retrieve her child. "Wow, Baby Yasmine really likes you! Hope you don't mind...where are *your* children? With your husband? *Oh*...you're not married, hmm? That's too bad..." (insert mock tragic air here) "But, *inshallah*, soon you'll have a nice young man come all the way to...where is it that you live, again?" Obviously, the absentee family member only makes further contact if her appearance in the photo is pleasing to him (to my Western and Westernized read-ers—hold your anger at this chauvinism until you hear what my friend Nermine once told me).

In terms of mothers getting involved, this can happen in many ways. In one, she notices the girl and breezily chats her up, so as to determine her eligibility. In another, she might befriend the girl and "try to fix her up" with the young men of the church (each of whom "turns out" to have a "glaring error" which might never be verified), after which she "gives up" and "jokingly" suggests her own son, instantly reneging (outwardly) while intensely scrutinizing the girl's reaction. Still others actually mention the fact that they're shopping for a daughter-in-law, and end up closer to the girl than their son is (before the marriage, anyway). In any of these cases (and others), the mother might be acting on her son's request, but she might also be taking the initiative. "But Sally," you might be wondering, "What if any of these instances plays out—and the wife-to-be has never even seen what the guy looks like?"

My swiftest response would be that in more recent years, and in more West-ernized cities, these shenanigans don't happen as often, since women are getting out of the house more, attending college, entering the work force, and meeting their own prospects. Like one of my best friends, who was the head of accounts in a Cairo hotel. Her now-husband met her upon check-in and proposed to her before he'd checked out, without having met her father (although he did make an appointment to meet him soon after).

Another response would be the answer my friend Nermine gave me at lunch one day, when I commented that a new member of our church was attractive. "Sally!!" she began (people seem to say that a great deal). "Looks aren't every-thing! Nor taste in cologne, nor being well-dressed, nor any of those things! The only important thing is if he treats you well." I said nothing, and reached for another piece of bread. "What do you think you're doing? Have you gone mad?" she asked, causing me to smirk inwardly and remark, "No, but *you* certainly have…" She shook her head and confiscated my freshly buttered roll. "Sally! Unmarried women aren't allowed to eat bread. Bread only makes you fat, and you can't be fat before the wedding." I sat up straighter. "Oh *really*," I said, giving her a keen look. "Of course. Men, and especially Egyptian men don't like their women to be overweight," she went on matter-of-factly.

"Wait, hold up. You're telling me to disregard a guy's appearance, his phy-sique or lack thereof, his *wealth* or lack thereof, *and* a face so unappealing that I would sooner adopt than reproduce—and on *top* of that *starve* myself and paint on a face so ghastly that even Dennis *Rodman* would cringe?"

She nodded placidly. "Your appearance must please the man, but it doesn't matter what *he* looks like, since he's the *man*," she finished, smiling beatifically. I, for the record, was *not* smiling.

Dating vs. Engagement

The period of engagement can last years or days, depending on the couple and their circumstances. In older times, the man would take years to save up and buy a house, before getting married—though these days, more and more couples get married at younger ages and just rent a flat somewhere.

In generations past, there were stringent limits as to what the engaged couple was allowed, in terms of time spent together, chaperones (or lack thereof), and physical contact. In the beginnings of this past century (1900s and beyond), love matches were rather rare, and the prospective bride and groom may not have ever spent time together or had a conversation. In some places, they may even have been betrothed since birth. In other places, the groom would look first towards his family, searching for a female cousin of marriageable age. The fact that these marriages were practically arranged obliterated long engagements and the subsequent "how far is too far?" question.

In later years, more and more love matches occurred, but only certain things were allowed the couple—going somewhere with a chaperone, talking on the phone for hours, having a visit under her father's roof. These days, things have gotten so Westernized (in places) that it's not unheard of for the engagement to follow the same course as a Western one (with the exclusion of sex—or so we hope). Which explains why a fair number of young Arab bachelors refuse to marry someone who was previously engaged. Though in more restricted circles, like the Saiid in Egypt, the engagement is still a rigorously monitored period of getting to know one another, devoid of holding hands and other, erm, goods-damagers.

In another show of the West's ideals having crept in, it's not that uncommon in the bigger cities for a girl to even have a "boyfriend" (this was not only unheard of, but strictly punishable 50 years ago, and so-called "honor killings" still happen today), although religion, the family's social station, and other factors may limit the girl's freedom (or increase it, as the case may be in more Western-ized cities).

I remember how surprised a cousin of mine was to watch her friend's wedding video, direct from Alexandria—"I can't believe this! They're doing the tango! Together!!" she gasped. "They're not half bad," I muttered, but she heard.

"That's the *point*, though!" she blustered. "They've obviously danced that same dance *before*—before they were *married!*"

Dating and Marriage Issues for Stateside Arabs

The rapidly morphing state of pre-marital relationships in the Middle East is exhausting, yes. But this next issue—the very same issues tailored to immigrants and first-generation Americans—is even more of a doozy. Especially since the meanings of the words "boyfriend," "girlfriend," "dating," "engagement," and "fiancé" mean so many things to so many people. In an earlier era, an American guy could take his "girlfriend" (a dame he was "seeing") out for a milkshake and a drive-in, with "should I try to hold her hand?" and "Is our third date too soon for a good-night kiss?" as the major questions at the back of his mind. A few years down the road, pregnancy outside of marriage was a big no-no, but everything was ok as long as it was kept under wraps. Fast forward yet a few more years, and people no longer cared to hide the fact that they were living with a significant other. And in recent years, young American women are *encouraged* to date many men, so they can find "that perfect someone" without "settling." More shocking these days (to the bumpkin from the "third world," anyway) is that it's practically commonplace for an American girl who's thinking about accepting a proposal to follow the advice of older friends who helpfully nudge her with "Try each other out" and "Why don't you live with him, honey? Just to make sure you can *live* with him, you know. So you can see if everything checks out."

Obviously, there are extremes in each direction, but it's taken for granted that there is a physical relationship between an American girl and her boyfriend, and that a guy has stayed over at his fiancée's house at some point. What used to be the exception is now the rule. But I'm not here to offer social commentary (lucky for you)—so we'll get on with the dating debate, shall we?

The first question asks *Should the young Arab American date?* While a Westerner might say "Sure, nothing to lose," an Arab—one following Arab precepts, anyway—would view dating as they would a snake—as something that could come back and bite them all later. In terms of Arab Americans, it's the parental set that would more readily think this way (unless they don't care about being respectable). They would not want their child to behave in a manner inconsistent with their (the parents') upbringing. Many of the most Americanized Arabs I have met have shrugged nonchalantly in the face of every topic I could throw at them—but they prickled at the word "dating." On the other hand, many immigrants are so intent on fully Americanizing that they really have no problem with allowing their children to go out. But more on them later.

So, shifting our focus onto the twenty-or thirty-something professional Arab American singleton who lives alone and can, for the most part, do what he or she likes, we run into a number of non-parentally motivated matters (strongly affected by whether the singleton identifies more as an Arab or as an American with Arab roots) which crop up when considering *if* (and how) they should date: *What do I want out of this, anyway?* and *Am I thinking ahead or for the moment?*

In the former, we find our singleton (not to be confused with "dating simpleton," although if the shoe fits…) making the decision between momentary physical satisfaction, the friendship which might provide the same physical satisfaction over a longer span of time, the casual date, the relationship that covers every aspect of one's life (but isn't really a high priority), the loving and amiable companionship that brings all of the pleasure and almost none of the guilt, or the less scaled-down version, which comes with more responsibilities and the same phone number, meaning that the options open to the young Arab American are the (so poetically named) "booty call," the "friend with rights," the "bookmarker," the "sometimes soul mate," the "unofficial spouse," or even the "live in love," respectively.

In the latter question, the singleton should definitely consider what effect his or her present actions will have on his or her future. For example, a girl who decides to "experiment" in high school or college will find herself with that many fewer choices, should she elect to marry an Arab. Also, while some people in smaller towns where everyone knows everyone might not flinch at getting engaged and then breaking it off if things don't match up well enough, other people see any broken engagement as a broken vow (I *did* mention that they signed a contract, right?) and would never marry someone who'd *broken* an engagement, apart from adultery or abuse. As mentioned before, a majority of American men would not exclude a potential mate just because she'd been engaged, in love—or erm, lust—before.

While never having dated might have its positive sides, there are a few negative aspects that can arise when one has literally never sat alone with a member of the opposite sex until the ripe old age of 22, 24 or 39. One issue is the singleton's not knowing how to act on a "date." Don't forget, our friend here has lived his or her life under the roof of a dark-haired and more fiery-tempered "father knows best" who, more often than not, has kept a tight rein on Junior's comings and goings. While this isn't a horrible issue, it can make for increasingly awkward and/or neurotic behavior on the part of the singleton. But it can also cause bigger problems, such as being too friendly, that is, not knowing enough about the opposite sex and "innocently" getting into situations (albeit unintentionally) that are better off avoiding. On the other hand, a singleton may feel the need to make up for lost time, whether in the quantity of dates he or she seeks (like Sara, who moved out of her father's house only to go out on dates every night), or in the "quality time" he or she spends with their date (like Marian, who went out with—and had a physical relationship with—the first guy she went out with after having moved out). Of course, some Arab Americans remember their upbringing and never forget that their first accountability is to God.

The next issue we come across is the question of *Whom should/can I date and/or marry?* While objectives and criteria may differ between recent immigrants and first generation Arab Americans, there are a few threads that tie them together. For example, one may choose to marry one in precisely the same circumstance, since a shared culture can ease things along. This is like the recent immigrant who wants to marry a girl from back home, so as to feel as though he's still at home, or possibly to have someone to commiserate with. One might also choose to marry one in precisely the opposite situation, such as the Arab American who has only been to the Middle East once, and wants to immerse herself in a culture that she was denied, and thus chooses someone who's fresh off the boat. Still others might choose a non-Arab, hoping for a less dramatic spouse, or perhaps a touch of culture. And of course, it goes without saying that some might marry an American citizen to obtain a Green Card, although as far as I know, these marriages last just as long as other marriages.

In terms of dating, some people might choose to date people from every category (immigrant, first-gen, American, non-Arab) in order to assess each category's feasibility as a marriage partner. Then again, some people might just want to experience everything before snapping on the old ball and chain.

In terms of inter-religious dating, neither Islam nor Christianity really supports it without some form of conversion, though obviously, different sects and denominations have different traditions. For example, Islam has a whole list of rules that a non-Islamic man has to follow before being allowed to marry a Moslem woman. Some of these rules include the changing of the non-Moslem name, the submission to a three-year period of scrutiny before being acknowledged as a true believer, the donning of the *Dishdasha* (which signifies having been "tamed into Islam") and the removal of his old life, as well as the more obvious ones like circumcision, a recitation of the Shahada, and a commitment to follow the Five Pillars of Islam.

The Coptic Orthodox Church also requires a conversion to their religion, though they go so far as to disavow any marriage that didn't occur in their church. Protestants, as well as many other Christians, however, have no such rule (although the Bible *does* warn against being "unequally yoked.").

Purity

Since we've already covered the "Arabic men want someone as pure as the driven snow" argument, this section will just explore the definition of purity, alternate views of such, extraordinary circumstances, and methods of dealing with the last two.

Merriam Webster defines purity as *"unmixed with any other matter; free from dust, dirt, or taint; spotless, stainless; characterized by no appreciable alteration; being thus and no other; free from what vitiates, weakens, or pollutes; containing nothing that does not properly belong; free from moral fault or guilt; marked by chastity; ritually clean."* Apparently, Arab men took Merriam Webster to heart, because many of them won't even look at a girl who's kissed another guy, although this view, as you can guess, is changing slightly in some places.

But right now we're focusing on Arabs in America, so let us ask the question *How far is too far?* The ideal answer is "Even less than one tenth of a step," but for some young people who've been brought up in the States, or for others who've recently escaped from the stringent limits of the Middle East, this option is less than ideal. I know that *some* people are bristling now, objecting to that remark and saying "I have *never* touched anyone!" or "My baby would never look at *any* person under the sun!" I know, I know, so kindly settle down and keep reading about the people who *aren't* as perfect as you and yours.

As we know, some people have done literally nothing. Ever. Next we find the ones who may have heard words of affection from someone, or said them, which is just as bad as having done something, to some people. Moving on, we run into those who have had the odd kiss here and there with the same person, whether based on lust or on actual emotions, then those who have shared the odd kiss with *more* than one. Sliding down the spiral we find those who've indulged in everything but actual "I could get pregnant, you know" sex (I call this the *Whorish Virgin Model*), those who had one monogamous relationship with someone "I thought I was going to marry!" Finally, we come across those who totally flout convention and go on to explore their sexuality, then feel that "what's done is done (so why stop now?)" known as *bayzah bayzah* in Arabic, turning to immorality as a lifestyle, since they're already ruined. I call this the *Tainted Flower Sce-*

nario. Tainted flowers, it should be noted, are in a league of their own and may as well invest in a scarlet letter to wear and a Salvation Army bell to ring, for all the support they'd get from fellow Arabs who learn about their way of life.

Of course, not all tainted flowers lose their self-respect and pull an Energizer Bunny stunt—some feel that it's important to get back to their "proper virginal status" and get sewn up in a patently Arab surgery, so that their husband would never know. I have dubbed this the *Third Wave Virgin Model,* mostly because a girl wouldn't have illicit relations just once, but she might twice ("one for the road" or whatever). Some Arabic women take this even further and pretend that they have no idea how to kiss.

Of course, not every act of immorality is an act of free will. In a sadder take on my previous models is the *Crushed Flower Model,* whereby a man seduces or attacks a woman, causing her to despair and leave her family rather than be killed by her father, turning her into a pliant wife because the man is "good enough" to take her in. Other times, a man might attack a woman so that she will be forced to marry him, granting him a Green Card/rich in-laws/etc. Still other times, the attack is used as a weapon against religious affiliation or political stance. Of course, Arab culture being what it is, the victim is sometimes blamed, and turned out of her house anyway. Other times, an Arab man, who may once have been so enamored of the girl he's decided on, might have to walk away (Arab men being the paragons of open-mindedness that they are). In any case, the woman is broken and the attacker benefits—or thinks he does. He certainly doesn't suffer, in many instances.

Moving right along, we come across the many methods that people employ to deal with "mistakes," no matter whose fault it is (interesting that men not *only* have no proof of virginity—apart from their word, which can be dubious—but even if they *aren't,* they're still seen as *men* and thus allowed to! What woman would walk away from a man for having slept around before having met her?) Anyway.

One method of getting fixed up hearkens back to the surgery (called *hymenorrhaphy* or *hymenoplasty*) that I hinted at earlier. This apparently makes the woman intact again, and the potential husband is none the wiser (woe to the virtuous woman who was a gymnast or horseback rider as a youngster and lacks a little something on her wedding night, though!). Moving on, we come across the highly arcane and technical strategy of *lying.* This obviously doesn't work all the time, as proven by the honor killings that still happen in some regions, and the post-honeymoon disownings that occur once the girl's father gets wind of it. Some women actually display a disregard for "the rules," doing what they want and depending on "love" to save them when their husband takes issue. Finally, some girls are forced to disregard the type of men who would care about provable virginity (interesting to note that some Western women who so fear the pain of their first time actually go under the knife—voluntarily—to surgically alter their virginity, in what's known as a *hymenectomy* or *hymenoclasis*).

What's There to Look Forward To?

In the home of an Arab (American or no), the greatest focus is on building a home and family. The master status is generally that of "parent," rather than "spouse," though this is, thankfully, changing.

The best feature of this child-centeredness is a cohesive family structure where the kids feel loved and everyone feels that they're a part of something greater. Another characteristic of the family of an Arab is lots of laughter! While Moslems are allowed divorce and the Orthodox and Catholics are granted annulments, divorces are sternly frowned upon in the Protestant church. This brings us to a minus regarding the whole "not divorcing" thing (no matter what religion the couple belongs to)—staying together can make for an Arctic climate if the parties should ever irrevocably disagree.

Furthermore, in Islam, we see that the man can "punish his wife" by 1-warning her, 2-withholding sex, and finally, if the other two don't work, 3-striking her lightly. This is interesting because 1-the sex is probably more rewarding for the man, anyway, and 2-striking, by definition, can't be "lightly done." I've dubbed this the *No More Nookie Model*, by the way.

Worse than no sex is the *Mrs. Arab Mathematician Model*, which came about when I read Geraldine Brooks' account of a Saudi man who denied his daughters and wife the chance to go to Harvard because he thought that going to America would corrupt them—not because America was bad (although he probably felt that way)—but because they "wouldn't know who they were anymore," which can be attested to by multitudes of first-generation Americans who hail from Arab countries and don't know whether they can or should date, drink, smoke, use drugs, go out after 8 p.m., or get their own apartment before they're married. Oh, but that's what we've been discussing for the past few pages, isn't it?

Finally is my conjecture that every married Arab woman alive grows to typify the *Yenta Principle*, which involves marrying everyone off, much like the mother-in-law in "Sense and Sensibility" (and the matchmaker in "Fiddler on the Roof," for whom this principle is named). Since these ladies have arranged their own lives already, they literally seek out young girls that they can mentor and marry off to young men that they know.

Singleness

Finally, despite the fact that matchmaking is a national past-time, and the fact that every Arabic song ever penned has to do with love—unrequited, forbidden, old or new, as well as aspects of love, such as faithfulness, loyalty and romance—it's far easier for a heretofore unattached Arab to go through his or her life wholly unattached (when compared with the average American, that is). Meaning single. Not that singleness is the norm for Arabs—most assuredly it is not. In fact, as we've discussed, Arabs love children and wish to marry and begin a family, but if they end up never having had one, they won't lament (the lack of spouse, anyway). This is because Arabs don't (or shouldn't, as we've seen!) have any experience dating, and thus "don't know what they're missing." This is not to say that they don't dream, or that they're happy to be single, just that they can be happy despite it, although some Arab divorcees may have been burned by a marriage, causing them to rejoice in their lack of commitment. As a famous proverb from Egypt says, *Illi yit'hireh bil shorba hayinfokh aala'l zabadi*, which means "The one who was burned by soup will blow on yogurt."

This totally differs from the "Wow, three months since the divorce—how do you cope?!" mentality that seems common in the West, or the "Who's next?" mentality that makes it seem as though having someone—anyone—is of utmost importance in being complete, in being validated by society and friends.

I know dozens of Arab 40-and 50-somethings who have never been married, either because their parents needed a caretaker, or because their job took up more time than a spouse could allow, or even because they couldn't find a decent candidate. And while they felt a certain sadness at never having had someone of their own, or a child in their image, they believed in and trusted God's will for their lives...

7

On Love—In Their Own Words

This next section was written by the Arabs I've met in my travels, as well as those that I befriended during my research for this book, not to mention the ones who lived in my town or state. Largely Egyptian, these Arabs span religions (sorry, no Druze, though), generations and situations (princes, poets and paupers, as it were). This is who they are and how they think about marriage and dating (underneath the changed names and details, anyway), in their own words, translated by me when needed (believe me, you'll be grateful), but otherwise unadulterated.

Egyptian women speak on what the Egyptian male wants in a wife

Tara, 28—"She has to be moral. If she's not a virgin on her wedding night, her husband gives her back to the father (in dishonor) and her father kills her or beats her and disowns her. Even today."

Sara, 18—"The lady must be of good honor and virtue. She shouldn't even have any male friends. We don't have the right to question them about their past, but should we tell them of even one kiss, they move on without a thought."

Laila, 40s—"A man wants an educated woman who is his equal in terms of education and status and social standing. He also wants her to be attractive (and, failing that, well put-together) and thin, since she's just going to get fat once the children arrive, which is no more than a year into it."

Nina, 24—"The man wants someone moral, someone beautiful(by his standards) and thin! When I got married, I was skinny and he was a thread! Now look at him! He's an ogre and I turned into a cow. I tell myself to lose weight, but then think, what's the point, if I'm just going to put it back on when I get pregnant again in one or two more years?"

How do people get married in Egypt?

Nada, 22—"Well, it's really very simple. He sees you, he asks about you, he comes over to your house and that's that. You should be engaged within the month. All that gazing and swooning? That's nothing. If he's interested in marriage, he'll come right over and not waste any time."

Tara, 28—"He sees you, and if interested, he'll inform you that you're to be engaged. This engagement can last a month, a year or even 10 years. The interest stage can also range in times. For example, a girl can smile to a man and be engaged the next day. (This is what happened to me). Or, he could take the safer route and ask about her, then obtain a photograph of her to show his family (if they're not readily available) and finally engage her. Egyptian engagement is roughly on par with American dating, only there's no sex."

Diana, 18—"Looks and expressions are very important in ascertaining whether he's interested or not. This can really drag for a long period, because some Egyptian men are a bit shy. After he gets the guts to talk to you, he asks to engage you and you sign a contract. This can be broken off but it's generally not the best idea to have too many broken engagements, or else people will think that you're either immoral or hopelessly flawed. Anyway, after the engagement comes the marriage, and that is the end of the story. You're locked in."

On Egyptian engagements.

Tina, 23—"The engagement is the only time you'll hear sweet words from your soon-to-be husband. Egyptian songs may be full of romance and longing, but that soon ends. After the engagement party, life is tougher, because then you feel like you have responsibilities and aren't as carefree, although you don't have to make such a big to-do about being virtuous after the engagement—the fish is hooked, so who cares?"

Faye, 40s—"In the engagement, you get to know each other. The limit of physical expression is set by the man, though there should never be any sexual goings-on. If he asks and she agrees, 9 times out of 10 he will consider the girl to be immoral and leave her—even if she lost her virginity with him. Kind of like going to the market and opening a lipstick to try the color, then putting it back and taking a closed one of the color you just tried."

Nabila, 33—"Having lived in America since I was about 16, I can tell you that it's better to get to know the potential match in a social setting before saying "yes." Less surprises than in the "traditional way," and you can see how he treats others and how they treat them."

Tara, 28—"Much affection is exchanged in this time, even though you can't take it further than that. But the affection is a good thing, because it forces you to create nice (non-physical) memories, since you can't cross the line. The memories are nice to think of later, when the marriage becomes what all Egyptian marriages are doomed to become—a non-romantic companionship where nothing ever happens. By the way, the most naughty men are the most pleased with the seemingly frigid fiancée. So play hard to get, girls!"

How did YOU meet your husband?

Nerdina, 21—"I was in church, he saw me, he asked about me and there you have it. We were engaged within the month."

Randa, 28—"I was working in a hotel and a tall man who had been a guest once before was checking out, when he asked if I was taken. We had never connected eyes before, so I was taken aback. At any rate, I told him that I wasn't. Then he told me that now I was. The engagement happened quickly, but I did not see him again for 6 months and actually forgot what he looked like. Now I wish I could forget what he looked like."

Carly, 25—"I grew up in Egypt and came over as a teenager. After seeing so many California-surfer-types, I longed for an Egyptian husband. I went back to Cairo and a guy from church asked for my phone number. I was so desperate to marry an Egyptian that I agreed right away and we got married. It was horrible, but that's another story."

What path does the Egyptian marriage take?

Tara, 28—"It's all romance and flowers till you get married. Then it's fight, fight, fight. Finally, you settle into a sort of friendship with the child as the common interest (all Egyptian marriages result in children). I tell you right now that if I didn't see Haleem for 6 months, I won't be sad. I wish I would get an opportunity to miss him, like in the old days."

Carly, 25—"They drop the act once you're married. Then they show their true colors, which usually aren't very pretty."

Faye, 40s—"A marriage is a way of establishing a home, yes, but it is important that there is something to draw the two together, whether it be chemistry, a shared profession, having grown up in the same town or region, a similar sense of humor…Romance isn't the be-all but there's a closeness and intimacy in our marriages that turns our relationship into an almost-blood relationship."

What limitations/inequalities are there for Egyptian women (in a marriage)?

Faye, 40s—"In every Egyptian marriage, the woman is the leaning wall that caves in. She has to, if she doesn't want to get abandoned or beaten. This isn't to say that she always agrees with the man, it's just that he's the one who gets his way in a fight."

Tina, 18—"The woman has to do what the man says."

Sam, 33—"It's no secret that I smoke and drink and drive around at all hours and do what I like—but my wife isn't allowed any of these things. I wouldn't let her even smoke a water pipe."

Ezzat, 28—"I think that the woman can do what she would like as long as the husband approves, and as long as she treats him with respect. It is important for us to choose someone who will be respectful."

Mina, 40s—"My wife is a doctor but from a very proud family, so I got around "ordering her" to stay home by trying to have children early on. When that didn't work, I bought a corporation that would fill her hours. She gets to stay home all day and do the financial things instead."

What is permissible for friends of opposing gender?

Ramses, 18—"I cannot be friends with girls, and especially girls my own age. For example, I can only be friends with you because you are 10 years older than I am. If you were younger and there was a chance…then no."

Elaine, 70s—"My daughter was punished for having ridden in a car once with her brother-in-law, even though she was a married woman at the time, the 70s. Her daughter, in the 90s went to a cinema with a man, once. She has fallen from the pedestal I have had her on since childhood. I can't forgive her for this shaming of the family, even if it was in America."

Heidi, 17—"I am not supposed to talk to boys, either online or on the phone. I do, however, and have gotten punished for it."

Egyptian mothers speak about their sons.

Ansaf, 40s—"My son is in his mid-twenties, and yet I cannot allow him to live alone, because of the temptations America has to offer. Also, he cannot date or have a girlfriend. This may seem cruel, but it's the only way to assure ourselves that he lives the way he would normally live had we brought him up over there."

Mary, 40s—"My son is in high school and to be honest, I'm concerned about him. Not just for morality's sake, but for goodness' sake. I'm concerned that he could drink, smoke, join a gang, use profanity, or leave his religion. America is so different than what we're used to and I know how kids are that age—they have to try everything. It would kill me to see him lose his culture."

American-born Egyptians speak about the "Egyptian Dating Conundrum."

Dayana, 20—"I have problems with Egyptian marriage, how they arrange you to a person you have never met before and they say MARRY HIM, YOU WON'T FIND BETTER—he has money, an apartment, a car and a very good job—and all their other stupid rules like dating—going out with a bunch of people, and what time you have to be home, they ask you when, where, why…"

Zara, 29—"I was born over there but came over before I learned to read, so I pretty much consider myself to be an American. My parents have vacillated a hundred times over whether I could date or not. Also, they've had significant reservations about my choice of friends over the years. At one point, I (a Copt) befriended a nice Moslem guy. I didn't realize what he wanted from me until it was too late. One second I was putting up with his awkward kisses, the next thing I knew, he was scratching, biting, choking and slapping me, telling me I would have to convert or die. I told him no, that I wouldn't. He ended up…attacking me, then proposing marriage. I was dumbfounded to realize that he'd planned the whole thing, down to the befriending. It turned out that he wanted a Green Card and didn't know how to find a "bride." Years later, I'm ruined and have ceased my search for an Egyptian guy who'll tolerate my "past." In fact, I wouldn't be telling you about this, except for the fact that I'm now living with a Greek guy who doesn't mind at all that I wasn't "virgin pure" when we got together."

Sally, 25—"I've always had a problem with my biculturalism. This is because I never knew what was what. It's not that I felt I had no identity, or that I couldn't come up with my own, it was that there was such a great divide about every-thing—and I always wondered "is this about culture, or did this come from the Koran or Bible? Is this 'unorthodox' or is it WRONG?" On one hand, many Americans said to 'try a guy on for size'(by dating, though more's acceptable these days) before committing, and the Egyptians said that dating was prohibited and you'd have to just get engaged to find out. That was a bit too Jane Eyre for me. (Mr. Rochester's doomed first marriage, recall…).

Not only that, but one culture said it was ok to be liberated, the other said that it was wrong. In Egypt, a woman isn't a second class citizen. She just isn't a man. Over there they don't see it as a bad thing, what women are, I mean. And what they can and can't do. In terms of dating, my dad's always said "no way!" but I've always had guy friends and hung out with them (women are too catty and com-petitive!). Truthfully, I've never once been tempted to take it further than a handshake or occasional hug—the whole "don't know what you're missing" thing, you know. For that, I'm grateful, coz I know that one breach would make it that much more difficult to draw the line, and to know where to draw it.

That said, I know I'll have a horrible time finding a husband that I can live with; on one hand, an American is too liberal for me (generally speaking), a fresh off the boat Egyptian is too conservative for me, an American born or there-abouts will likely be more Americanized than I am, and if they're not then I'll think they're wannabe Egyptians."

Nelly, 18—"I don't see what the issue is. I grew up the Egyptian way, but don't see anything wrong with kissing and boyfriends and stuff. I've never had any of that stuff, but at the same time I don't get offended when I see that, or a miniskirt or tank top on TV. Or in real life…I think I'll marry someone who was born here, like me."

Egyptian men in America—what they want in a wife, and their thoughts about her morals.

Samuel, 27—"I want a wife who is beautiful and smart and very moral. And if I can take the Green Card, that would also be nice."

Naseem, 33—"I can't stress enough how important the morals are. If a girl kisses a man she wasn't married or engaged to, that's it. The girl should always respect herself and others. I, however, like extracting kisses from innocent girls. So it makes me wonder, because most Egyptian men are like me, and yet the girls have "never been kissed." Do the math! Someone's lying!"

Mohammed, 29—"I don't care THAT much if she's virgin or not, because I know that she could do 100 other things and still technically be a "virgin." But that's not the point. I am a very sexual man and I expect my wife to be the same. If she's virginal then maybe she didn't care about sex to experiment, in which case I don't want her. I may live in Los Angeles now, but I've always thought this way."

Sam, 24—"I think it's important that she be in great physical shape and stay that way! You know the freshman 15? Well, there's something also called "the Egyptian 80." And all this talk about being moral? Who really cares what happened pre-wedding? It's what happens after that counts. Also, even if a girl swears up and down to be "pure," then she could be lying and have had the surgery, or even just messed around in every possible way. And to me, a liar is worse than a slut."

Ashraf, 29—"I was engaged to a very beautiful Egyptian girl from America, Zara. I was so happy because she was gorgeous and perfect, but then she admitted that she had been attacked in college. And by a Moslem! This is unacceptable to me. We Copts and Moslems don't really get along all that well. But apart from that, I would always have had to remember the police report photos that I saw-bite marks, bruises, etc. I would always have wondered if she was crying in pleasure or pain when they happened. Couldn't she have fought a little harder? Couldn't she have done something? Part of me even thinks that she didn't mind it so much, or maybe even wanted it. Didn't she know what men are capable of? I tell you, it's plagued me since our breakup. I thank God that she told me before we got married. We still keep in touch—we were very close, you know. And also, her parents have cut her off…when they found out about it, they blamed her (despite her injuries) and said she asked for it by being friends with a boy. I figure that at least I can be her friend, now that she's an orphan…"

American-born Egyptian men—what they want in a wife, and thoughts about her morals.

James, 26—"She can't have had a boyfriend before! I don't care if he was internet or not, she's outtie if she did!"

Albert, 19—"Of course I prefer a moral girl—who doesn't? But I understand that mistakes do happen, and that people date when they're younger. So if she had changed, I'd forgive her."

Miscellany.

Tamer, 28—"In Egypt, most Egyptians marry by a different way than in the past—for example, in the past the woman cannot see her man until they marry, and also her husband is supposed to meet her father first and sometimes they did not know each other—the man and the woman, I mean, but he just comes to her father coz he heard about her, that she is a good woman, so he introduces himself to her family. But today there are so many differences, like before anyone get married they must know each other and be interested in each other before he can introduce himself to her, and after that they can marry."

Elias, 29—"I lost my family to the Israelis—through both eviction and gunfire. Now I'm alone, with a younger sister and that's all. But she's married and doesn't have time for me—or my anger. I want to get married so badly—I've only had three relationships in my life (like the dating or girlfriend kind) and they all fell through because I wanted too much. Oh, I never pushed them into anything, I just wanted to get married as soon as I felt something for them. At the time, I figured it was because I loved them, but I've come to realize, recently, that I just want to have a family again. My mistake was in choosing American women, who found me "clingy," not realizing that in an Arabic marriage, there's no "space." You're together every waking moment, you're companions, and you don't take a vacation FROM your spouse, you take one WITH them. Right now, I've met a Lebanese girl who's beautiful and seems—*inshallah*—to be marriage material. But, once bitten, twice shy, so…"

8

Language and Other Issues in Linguistics

Out of all of the issues present in someone's acculturation into a new place—or their fitting into the place where they've grown up—language is the most inescapable. After all, one can go his or her entire life without dating, without working, without having opinions, even, but if he's to haggle over a car, he should be able to speak the same language as the car salesman. If she's to order a pound of calf liver and *not* sheep's eyes, she has to be able to tell the butcher in a language that he can understand. Granted, there are places in America that have salesmen and butchers who speak Arabic—and doctors and lawyers, too. There are even entire communities where Arabic flows more freely than any other language. But not every Arab American has the luxury of living there.

And so. Here we go, to examine different aspects, anecdotes and phenomena of verbal communication and the Arab American.

Arabic

It's never enough to identify one as "an Arabic speaker"—there are entirely too many dialects!

Afro-Asiatic languages are broken up into the following categories: Berber, Egyptian, Chadic, Omotic, Cushitic, and Semitic languages. This last one is the most important one for our purposes, though *not* because its languages range from the Biblically-mentioned yet now-extinct Phoenician, Amorite and Akkadian, to the still-strong Aramaic, Maltese, and Ethiopian, among others. Rather, Semitic is an important category because it houses the smaller group of Central Semitic languages, under which Arabic falls.

Arabic can be broken up into five somewhat geographically segregated dialects. Starting at the most Western section of the Arabic world, we see *Western*

Arabic (*Maghribi*), affected by the Berber language and spanning Morocco, Algeria, Tunisia, Mauritania and Libya. Moving along to Northeastern Africa we find the *Egyptian and Sudanese* Arabic, with influence derived from the Turkish language as well as the Coptic (Ancient Egyptian) and Nilotic (modern-day Kenyan, Congolese, Ethiopian, Tanzanian and Ugandan) languages. Next up we run into *Levantine Arabic*, which is influenced by Aramaic and other Biblical languages, and spoken in Lebanon, Syria, Palestine and Jordan. Moving northward, we come across *Iraq*, with Arabic affected by Farsi, Turkish, and the local Semitic languages of Chaldean (Aramaic) and Assyrian. Finally, a downward swerve takes us into the *Arabian Peninsula*, where Bedouin dialects and the now-extinct Southern Arabian languages have affected the dialect.

In a yet more-encompassing breakdown, we can consider every country beginning with Egypt and to the East as a speaker of *Eastern Arabic*, and all of the African countries, from Libya to Morocco, speakers of *Western Arabic*.

American English

As you may have deduced from the preceding section, there are a few differences between different Arabic dialects, and *more* than a few differences between English and Arabic—syntax, sentence structure, grammatical rules, vocabulary. But there are almost as many differences between American English and British English, British being the dialect that most Arab countries teach. So an American might wonder why a British friend's car has a "boot" and a "bonnet," not realizing that the boot isn't footwear and the bonnet's not a hat. By the way, "boot"= trunk and "bonnet"= hood, for you provincial types. By the same token, an immigrant might just be the slightest bit confused when asked to use the elevator, even if he's ridden a "lift" a thousand times.

But having spoken a different English back home isn't the only challenge that an immigrant can face; sometimes the English learned wasn't correct in the first place, whether because the speaker misspoke, or because the listener misheard. An example of this dates back to the days when I first met one of my favorite families ever: The parents were both reviewing word lists for their medical licensing exams, and I had come over to hang out, mainly, and offer any translations they might need.

We discussed many things that evening—the economic state of their town in Egypt, their respective medical practices, and the new Mostafa Amar record. Then we discussed the temporary jobs they'd taken. "You have a degree in psychology, hmm?" said Dr. D., the family's patriarch. I nodded, rather hesitantly, I admit—many times, an Egyptian or Arab might ask "Are you free tomorrow?" or "You're good at refinishing cabinets, aren't you?" before laying out a heavy request. In this case, I was afraid to be charged with psychoanalyzing all of our mutual friends, or worse yet, someone in the room. Instead, though, Dr. D. proceeded to tell me all about a man who'd come into the hospital that day.

"Sally, I think he was psychic," he began. I couldn't suppress the lifting of my eyebrow, but I kept my voice neutral. "Oh?" I tossed out. He nodded vigorously, and so did his wife, so I settled deeper into my chair, prepared for a drawn-out tale involving tea leaves, crystal balls and beaded curtains. Instead, however, Dr. D. said "He was psychic! He started yelling at the nurses, without having been provoked! He fought the orderlies until the police came!" A breath. Then, dramatically, a final declaration—"He was psychic!"

The eyes of his wife and children on him, he bowed his head and was still (I wondered if it would be appropriate to applaud). "How do you say it in English," his wife asked—"Mad? Crazy?" I barely stifled a giggle as I said "Oh! *Psycho*! The man was psycho, not *psychic*!"—It turned out that they were familiar with the term *psychotic* and had misheard the more slangy *psycho* as psy*chic*, causing more than a few rounds of laughter that evening—especially when I explained the actual meaning of the word *psychic*, and the living stereotypes prevalent in America.

Another factor that can contribute to the misunderstandings between foreigners and Americans is *accent*. On one hand, Americans sometimes describe foreigners—even English-speaking ones like the British—as "talking funny," with only Americans as the true and "proper" English-speakers (this assertion is very funny to the British, most of whom speak much more proper English, but anyway). On the other hand, American accents vary greatly from one another, from Southern to Midwestern to Valley Girl—and everything in between. Both instances heighten the language barrier, because the immigrant feels misunderstood, as in the first case, and has difficulty understanding this strange (to him or her) English—whether spoken by characters on TV, by their supervisor at work, or by the clerk at their local supermarket.

Compounding the accent issue is the fact that some only have a "book knowledge" of English and can't understand any of it, whether spoken by other Arabs—in which case they most definitely could never connect their American friends' English to a meaning—or by the voice in their head, in which case they have a problem. But that's just the beginning.

Never having practiced in an American setting might result in shyness or a lack of confidence, further resulting in keeping silent, even at the grocer's. Having learned English from a media source (books, tapes, films) may result in a somewhat dated set of colloquialisms—the datedness can be from an era, like "the '70s" ("Yeah, maaaan") or "the '50s"("Be there or be square!")—although in a reverse of this very phenomena, I learned the Arabic that my parents brought over, and consequently get cooed over by Arabs who find my *"shokran gazeelan"* to be an endearing, if outdated, expression of thanks. Almost worse—er, more amusing—than speaking dated English could be movie slang, like "Excellent!" from "Bill and Ted's Excellent Adventure," or "I'm the king of the world!" from "Titanic," or even "NOT!" from "Wayne's World."

Accent vs. Understanding

Another factor that can positively or negatively affect the Arab's attempts to speak with non-Arabs is the *perceived understanding* factor.

To illustrate this, let me share two different tales with you—the first involved a (very) nice-looking Egyptian who had lived in America for about 10 years, since his 19th birthday. He looked mega-Coptic; his build, his hair, the set of his eyes. I could imagine one of my titled forefathers—maybe Ramses the Great or Amen-hotep?—having passed such sleepily seductive eyes on to this lad. At any rate, I had admired him from afar (he went to a church I once attended) for half a year without having made any signal that he was allowed to approach (his eyes told me that the admiration was mutual). After all, he wasn't married, I wasn't married—if I so much as said his name, every Egyptian in my acquaintance would be around my neck, trying to engineer a merger with him. If I even threw the slightest hint of interest at him—a smile, the lift of an eyebrow—I knew he'd be at my side in an instant (I had noticed that in this, too, he was giving me the same treatment—the "couldn't be bothered" treatment that's an instant red flag signaling attraction between Arabs) and for a while, I had no wish of that. For now, I wanted to preserve the mystery that his eyes perpetuated.

Until one day, when I overheard him chatting with the pastor. I had never heard his accent in English before then, and I must say that it was almost perfect. Just enough foreignness to be intriguing, but not enough that one couldn't understand him. No *"Za beebels want dreenk Bibsi Kooola"* from this lad! I decided that I had to talk to him, so I went looking for my own glass of "Bibsi Koola" ("Pepsi Cola," to you provincial types). A girlfriend of mine came up to comment about my dress, which I must concur looked very chic. "I know," I responded, with a haughty lift of my eyebrows.

My pseudo-snobby expression must have been amusing, because she burst into laughter, and I joined in. Lifting my eyes a bit, I realized that he, the ultra-Copt with the bedroom eyes, had been watching me. My smile disappeared, though a moment later I decided that the situation was actually comical, and smiled at him, if briefly. Not a second passed before, eyes glued to mine, he handed his coffee cup to the good Reverend and made his way over to me.

"Hullo, Ashraf," I began, dropping the smile and nodding at him once. "Do you realize that the bouquet of flowers in your face surpasses the flowers of the field?" he asked me in Arabic (Egyptians are not only poets, but cool with the lines). I imagine that a shy smile accompanied the drop of my eyes, and I changed the subject. I asked him about work, his family, and all of the expected (and safe!) topics. The moment an English word crept into my speech, he shifted into English, too, much to my dismay (Ashraf had a gorgeous speaking voice, but especially when he spoke Arabic).

At first, I kept my speech slow enough that any second-language English speaker could follow along, though he soon made it clear that I didn't have to slow down on his account. So I started speaking as I usually did in English, both in speed and vocabulary. Within the first minute, however, I realized the folly in my ways—sure, he was great at deciphering English and registering slang, but his actual *vocabulary*, I'm sorry to report, was very lacking. He actually apologized for it, and asked me the meanings of about eight words that I'd used. Then he asked if we could get together one evening and discuss vocabulary with my parents, but that's another story for another time.

Speaking of other stories, I owe you another one that will illustrate the other side of what I just, erm, illustrated—how accent can sometimes affect our perception of the speaker's understanding (I won't mention the fact that every Arab I speak to slows down once they hear my accent, it would just upset me).

The reverse of the Ashraf-tale involves a close friend of mine, Sherine. Before leaving Cairo and moving to America in the late 60s, Sherine was educated in medicine. Despite never having practiced in America, she continued to read up on her field, among other things, in both English and Arabic. Thirty years in America and three children who excelled in English helped Sherine become near-perfect in the language, speaking with so mild of an accent that she could never have been pegged as an Arab. Her children, however, never accepted her firm grasp on the English language, going as far as explaining and translating the nightly TV news program for her, even now, three decades after having moved here (much to her—and my—amusement).

Moving on, we find that some Arabs who move to the States never actually learned English back home and thus can't speak it. This has a number of effects on the immigrant, most notably the self-imposed isolation, the embarrassment or shyness, and the hindrance during a job-search or hunt for new friends (a little xenophobia, anyone?).

Bilinguals

As we've discussed, language is a very important part of anyone's life, but especially those who live amid two or more cultures. First-gens who speak Arabic are usually viewed very favorably, and thus feel pride in their accomplishment. Some first-gens are so rooted in their bilingualism that they can not only pick accents up easily, but actually slip into them when stressed or nervous. One Egyptian girl told me that she'd noticed that she tends to "slip into an Arabic accent when speaking English to Arabs, and a Saiidi accent when speaking to Saiidis in Arabic. I guess I'm subconsciously trying to help them understand me."

A Moroccan guy I knew in college spoke Saudi to a mutual friend, and Egyptian to me. A Moroccan girl in the same college spoke Egyptian Arabic so well that I actually wondered if she had grown up in Egypt. Yet another Moroccan lady I met in the shopping mall one day asked me where I was from, then proceeded to speak Egyptian Arabic for about five minutes before I realized that she was actually Moroccan. I found it fascinating that three different Moroccans that I met in three different years could replicate my dialect so well. I found it a bit disheartening that I could neither replicate nor even understand their Arabic with any semblance of skill, and, to this day, wonder why the dialects from Morocco all the way to the Gulf all count as Arabic, when they're so different.

One thing American Arabic speakers of all dialects *do* have in common is their classification into one of Charles Osgood's categories of *coordinate* and *compound* bilinguals. A *coordinate bilingual* is one who has "*learned their two languages in different contexts; one language is learned at school…whereas the other is spoken at home,*" while *compound bilinguals* learn both languages in the same situation, and can control any interference (such as my being able to stick to pure Arabic when speaking to a friend in Egypt who doesn't speak any English), but more on interference in a bit.

Another set of categories regarding bilingual first-generation Americans concerns the activity level of bilingualism: *active bilinguals* can (and do) understand and speak both English and Arabic, and *latent bilinguals* find themselves understanding the language, despite a deficiency in speaking it with any amount of frequency (either because of preference or lack of skill). If this is getting too technical for you, skip the next section, coz you ain't seen nothing yet!

Moving right along, yet another distinction between bilinguals lies in their knowledge (or not) of grammatical rules, and their ability to point out grammatical mistakes (or lack thereof): The *naive bilingual* carries some grammatical rules from one language (let's say English) over to their speech of the other language (Arabic, in this example). Like the speaker who might say "*ana akalt khadra salata*" ("I ate green salad," respectively and literally) when the correct grammar would be "*ana akalt salata khadra*" ("I ate salad green," respectively and literally, since the adjective—*khadra*—comes after the noun—*salata*—in Arabic), or the one who might assert that "*ana akhadt helween sowar*" ("I took pretty pictures," literally. I disagree, though—I've never met an Arab who takes anything other than perfectly centered, perfectly *boring* photos. Apart from me, that is…) rather than the grammatically correct "*ana akhadt sowarr helween*" ("I took pictures nice," literally and respectively, although this is correct grammar for Arabic). The *sophisticated bilingual*, on the other hand, knows the rules of the language, and is able to identify grammatical errors (even if he or she makes them).

Back to interference, which I mentioned above, Aleya Rouchdy, assistant professor in the department of Near Eastern languages and literature at Wayne State University, identifies three types that bilingual first-gens execute in her "Research on Arab Child Bilinguals." The first is the *translation of English items word for word*, such as "I didn't say"—incorrectly "*ana mish olt*," fitting "*mish*" ("not," meaning "didn't") and "*olt*"("said"), which should actually be "*ana ma oltish*," although "*ana mish olt*" can actually be used to mean "Didn't I say?"

The second type of interference is the *modification of an item*, allowing it to fit into the recipient language's pattern. This hearkens back to "*mi'tenshinna*," which you'll recall was a construct meaning "stressed" or "under tension," since "*mi-*" is a prefix denoting that the connected verb applies to the person or thing that one's discussing. So, as "*mi'aas'laga*" means "stuck," "*mi'karkiba*" means "cluttered," and "*mi'lakhbata*" means "messed up," this modification is responsible for such gems as "I have to buy some *magalas* for school," ("*magala*" is the singular for "magazine," "*magalaat*" is the plural, so adding an "s," as in English, allows the word to fit into an English phrase), "*iftikri il* necklasat," ("Remember the necklaces," taking the English "necklace" and adding the Arabic pluraliser "-*at*," so that "necklace" fits into the Arabic sentence—don't ask me where that sentence came from, by the way).

Finally, we come upon the *retaining of items without translation* (meaning throwing a word of *one* language into the *other* language when unsure of the translation), which Rouchdy claims only happens from English to Arabic, such as "*ana kont aayza arohh l'il* candy store," ("I wanted to go to the candy store"), although I, for one, have said things like "What I want, *yaani*, is to feel as though you *bit'heb'ooni*," where "*yaani*" means "like" or "I mean" (and is NOT the moniker of the long-haired New Age musician, despite what you might think) and *bit'heb'ooni* means "you all love me."

A less technical going-on in terms of language and first-generation Americans is when he or she might learn the incorrect meaning of a word, either because of someone else's misuse or the first-gen's own misunderstanding. Other less technical notions that I myself have come up with are the *Sunflower Seed Model*, which predominantly concerns first-generation Americans who are sophisticated compound bilinguals of the active nature, meaning they speak Arabic almost as often and as well as they do English.

These linguists know thousands of words in both languages, but they fall short of certain words that they learned in their weaker language and not the stronger. The theory gets its name because I've always known what "*libb*" look like, how they smell, taste, feel and sound—and yet, for years, I never knew the English name for these snacks. Finally, when—and only when—a clan of immigrants came calling, they asked what "libb" were called in English. Aghast at the fact that I, an "American," had no idea, they asked around and I asked around and we finally compared notes and agreed that "*libb*" were a sunflowerish-type seed (although they're actually closer to pumpkin seeds). Hence the name ("*Pumpkin Seed Model*" sounded too Halloweenish, I thought).

Another amusing phenomena in the lingual sector is the *Open-Light Model*. This phenomena is witnessed when a person translates *everything* from their more commonly-used language into their less-commonly used language—carrying entire idioms over—with examples that are more often than not hilarious. The model takes its name from the fact that I (and many, if not most, English-speaking Arabs) have never once asked someone to "turn the light on" in English—rather, the request is "Please open the light," which is derived from "*iftah il nour*," Arabic for the same words. This is because asking "*walaa'ii il nour*," while literally correct, means "Please light the light," meaning, I suppose, "Turn the flames on." Another example of this takes us to the post office, where "*hanirmii il gawabat*"—that is, where we'll go to "throw the letters."

9

From Traveler to Immigrant—Styles of Assimilation

This chapter differs from the others in that Arabs, whether immigrant, first-or second-generation, won't necessarily have the inside track on what I'll be telling you (though most of it's common sense which any well-read individual could come up with off the top of his head, sort of), which begins at culture shock (which doesn't *just* have to do with overseas holidays), then meanders on to acculturation styles, ending up with some discussion as to what America's "melting pot" status really means (although everything's up for discussion).

Culture Shock

Overseas-living guru R.L. Kohls defined culture shock as:

> *the term used to describe the more pronounced reactions to the psychological disorientation most people experience when they move for an extended period of time into a culture markedly different from their own. For some people, the bout with culture shock is brief and hardly noticeable. For others, it can cause intense discomfort, often accompanied by hyper-irritability, bitterness, resentment, homesickness and depression. In some individuals, culture shock may be accompanied by distinct physical symptoms of psychosomatic illness.*

What this basically means is that the term *culture shock* is the name given to a temporary time of "freaking out" that oftentimes happens when a person moves to or holidays in a place whose culture isn't the same as his or hers, so mild (in some) as to go unnoticed, then again so severe (in others) as to cause a wide range of symptoms, both physiologically and psychologically.

The four official stages of culture shock are: the *tourist (honeymoon) phase,* the *cultural shock (crisis) phase,* the *adjustment, reorientation, and gradual recovery phase,* and finally, the *acculturation (adaptation or resolution) phase.*

The *honeymoon* phase is characterized by excitement, interest and optimism about the trip (or marriage, as the case may be), finding things to be quaint or charming. The next phase, *cultural shock,* feels like "Oh my *GOSH,* what have I gotten myself into?"—molehills turn into mountains, and the "*My,* that's quaint" mentality shifts into "I ate *WHAT*?!" The traveler feels fearful, depressed, anxious and disenchanted, complaining more than he or she usually might (woe to those who live with people who complain a lot!) possibly suffering from hypochondria or even psychosomatic ailments. In the *adjustment* phase, things start to make sense, and the traveler regains his or her sense of humor, starts exploring things with more confidence, putting things into perspective. Finally, the acculturation phase finds our friend understanding and accepting things ("Oh, eyeballs are a *delicacy,* Mom, didn't you know?"), regaining interest and finally integrating into his or her surroundings.

Michael Winkelman of Arizona State's anthropology department writes that "*the phases are both sequential and cyclical. The shift from crises to adjustment and adaptation can repeat as one encounters new crises, requiring additional adjustments. One may become effectively bicultural, and then the adaptation phase is a permanent stage.*"

As one can guess, culture shock can negatively affect an individual, in the form of *stress reactions* (stress lowers immunity, sometimes causing or allowing illness, whether psychological or psychosomatic), *cognitive fatigue* (the "too much information" thing, which can overload one's circuits and effect a meltdown), *role shock* ("Who am I? What do they expect me to *do*?") and *personal shock* ("Wow, they have that here? I've always wanted to try it…" all the way to "Good *gracious,* if that happened back home, someone would have arrested them a *long* time ago!").

Winkelman offers some strategies for coping, such as *pre-departure preparation* (reading up on the culture, finding out where the most disparity between your and their culture lies), making *transition adjustments* (maybe snagging a traveler's phrasebook, finding ways to speak one's own language, whether with fellow sojourners or even calling friends back home), *creating and maintaining personal and social relations* (again staying in touch with friends and family from back home, as well as trying to pick up some friends in the new place), *discerning cultural and social interaction rules* (including communication, thought, negotiation or management) and finally, *gaining conflict resolution and intercultural effective-*

ness skills (realizing that problems occur everywhere, and finding out ways to solve them in one's new setting).

Finally, for those lucky (or unlucky, as the case may be) enough to return "home," there are a number of things to keep in mind. First of all, if one's been away for a long time, things may have changed, maybe even drastically (my mother's always shocked to hear how Alexandria's changed since our last trip there a few years ago). This may lead to a belief that one doesn't belong "back home" anymore, especially if one's old friends have moved on and/or aren't all that keen on hearing about his or her travels. This might make the longing for the friends one made abroad even sharper. A number of sources point to *planning* as the best way to avoid this clash of re-entry; planning what one will do upon return, and how one will pay for it. Another suggestion is that the traveler try to stay up-to-date on the happenings back home.

A horribly tacky (but nevertheless valid) example of this is the college student who's had to miss out on "Days of Our Lives" (or whatever soap opera is all the rage right now) for an entire semester, and comes back from university only to find that Stefano escaped (again), Bo and Hope renewed their vows and are expecting (again) and John Black still hasn't had a genuine facial expression (no one ever thought it would happen, anyway—and that's a fact!). So, if our friend from college had faithfully read "Soap Opera Digest," she wouldn't be suffering from the clash of re-entry (I did warn you).

Berry's Acculturation Styles

Moving on, we glance the four acculturation styles set forth by acculturation demi-god John W. Berry—*marginalization, assimilation, integration and separation*—which house four different strategies that immigrants (and sojourners) have for coping with a new setting:

Integration is when a person who's moved to another land has embraced some customs from the new place and kept some from the old. *Assimilation* is when the immigrant "forgets" his or her old ways and fully embraces the new. *Separation* is the reverse, when the immigrant shuns the new customs in favor of his or her homeland's. Finally, *marginalization* is the rejecting of both old *and* new. For the record, I feel as though I exist in all four styles—simultaneously (does anyone else?).

An *integrated* woman might cook grape leaves and spaghetti (not together, I hope), listen to Abdel Halim and John Tesh (why?!), and have both American and Arab friends.

An *assimilated* man might marry an American lady, refuse to speak Arabic, throw out his Omm Kalsoum collection and only eat at Outback Steakhouse (I certainly hope he's taking his Lipitor).

A *separated* Arab American might refuse to learn English and balk at any restaurant that doesn't have "Ali" or "Aladdin" in the title.

And a *marginalized* person apparently is neither Arabic nor American, which I can't even begin to imagine (no, I won't do it!).

The Great "Melting Pot"

Nowhere does it state that for foreign-born Americans to "integrate," they'd have to forget their culture and traditions. Peter Salins, in his *Assimilation, American Style*, says he feels that this belief is an example of the "up or out" model. That is "*either immigrants bring themselves 'up' to native cultural standards, or they are doomed to live 'out' of the charmed circle of the national culture.*" He goes on to suggest that the "melting pot" analogy that's so popularly spouted is a farce, since everything in the cauldron would melt into one great stew—each person or culture maybe changing the brew marginally, but ending up with the same chemical (or cultural, as the case may be) composition, which Americans definitely don't have. He goes on to postulate that the constituents of the brew would be "irreversibly changed," sort of like in the "*most aggressively assimilationist period, the "Americanization" movement of the '20s and '30s,*" which might explain why modern second-and third-generation Arabs almost never speak Arabic and oftentimes have no grasp of their cultural heritage—making books such as this one very helpful in their search to find themselves.

Assimilationism, which advocates a melting together of everything into only *one* thing, is the opposite of cultural pluralism (the theory that *all* cultures should exist, rather than assimilating, hence the word "opposite"). Through the lens of the cultural pluralist, American culture would be likened to a salad bowl, where becoming part of the mixture didn't mean that the ingredients had to morph into something they *weren't*, or give up something they were. Rather, each ingredient brings something different to the dish, adding that much more variety and flavor to it, while remaining (largely) unchanged (apart from the fact that each ingredient is identified as being part of the salad).

This is the model that I recommend Arab Americans take; for our own sake, since separated Arab Americans tend to have a hard time living here, and more so, because our Arabic heritage and traditions are too precious to fade with the waves of Westernization that keep battering the Middle East. Our culture is also too beautiful *not* to share—and sharing who we are will only help to preserve our traditions!

While some might fear "losing their culture," (which I've seen on many different occasions, actually) an important thing to remember is that becoming more American and becoming less Arabic aren't mutually exclusive. Just because someone learns about American culture and lives it, in some ways, doesn't mean that they have to *stop* doing what they've done (i.e., what makes them an Arab), or believing what they've believed their whole lives. Learning as much as possible about every option (while remembering and respecting one's history) and then making an informed and educated decision is a great way to ensure that one makes the best possible choice. After all, every culture has *some* bad things in it, and why hold on to things that will only end up hurting us?

10

A New Life—Challenges That Immigrants Face

I can't think of anything sadder or more heart-wrenching than packing up and leaving one's homeland forever. Except, maybe, the impossible task of trying to fashion a *new* life in the image of the old and having little to work with. In this chapter, we will have a look at the challenges that immigrants commonly face upon moving to America, and in the next, we'll meet people who have faced them.

New Challenges

Most people aren't independently wealthy, and certainly not Arabs. While there is a pervasive stereotype of the Saudi sheikh coming to America and spending money as though it were rainwater, the truth is that in many Middle Eastern countries, per capita income is something like $2,000 to $4,000 U.S.—and that's in the richer countries. Be that as it may, there are obviously *some* millionaires and some countries, in fact, which don't have many (if any) poor people. But what happens when these comfortably-living Arabs move to America? After one figures in the $1,000 to $2,000 airfare (per person) from the Middle East, the freight/moving costs (don't even want to venture a guess), hotel and land transportation, first month's rent and deposit (and further security deposit for not having any credit in the U.S.) as well as food, the sojourner is in pretty sad shape (unless his bank balance was something like 47 billion to begin with, in which case I have no pity at all).

This is all before the rate of exchange, by the way, which (for example) is seven Egyptian pounds to one U.S. dollar right at the time of this printing. To give you some idea as to what a pound can buy in Egypt, consider the fact that a Pepsi is about one Egyptian pound, a popular cassette is about 10 pounds, and a nice pair of shoes is around 150 (as opposed to the prices that I grew up with—.50, 5 and 90 pounds, respectively).

So. Not only has our immigrant lost his shirt in relocation expenses, he's also moved to a place where the standard of living is higher (probably in quality, many would venture, but definitely in terms of cost). On top of that, the immigrant usually doesn't have a job to report to from the get-go. But what about doctors and dentists and other people who could most definitely start their own clinics, catering to people of their nationality, you might be asking. Oh, how innocent you are, dear reader. America has built a reputation for having high standards in everything, including medicine. This means that even if Dr. Ahmed from Lebanon has just taken his board exams in Beirut, he still has to take them again here. But most people don't take their board exams there only to have to retake them upon arrival—no, a majority of immigrants are established in their fields, causing them to revisit subjects they haven't thought of in many years. The studying takes hundreds of hours, but worse yet is the fact that many immigrants have to simultaneously work in menial jobs to support themselves and their families. An example of this is the family of Dr. Botros.

Dr. Botros brought his wife, Maha, and their two college-aged children to America one year ago. Botros's specialty is radiology, while Maha's is cardiology. Or should I say their specialties "were"—that's right, they left thriving practices behind in Cairo, in hopes of giving their children a chance at a better education. So now, this cardiologist who owned three clinics, and his Chief of Cardiac Surgery wife are reduced to working 10-hour days as lab technicians, spending their free time immersed in studying for their upcoming physician's licensing exams. On top of that, Maha has taken it upon herself to become fluent in English, attending weekly classes at the local college. But that brings us to another point.

Language. As we learned in Chapter Eight, one's lingual skills (or lack thereof) can make (or break) his or her status as a job-seeker. One's weakness in English can limit the social contacts available to him or her, resulting in an immigrant who suffers from self-perpetuating loneliness and alienation.

Which brings us to our next point, *friendships.* While not *every* town has people of the immigrant's nationality, it's important for him or her to find people of a similar culture, so that cultural distinction and ethnic integrity are maintained. At the same time, it's important to make social contacts with those from the new culture—in this case, Americans. This is because a member of a minority who surrounds him-or herself with a community of like-minded people and yet attempts to live in the dominant culture will have problems later on. The new language suffers, the children suffer (if they come into contact with American kids, anyway), and in general, one will live in a bubble. This is fine if there are enough fellow Arabs around, but what if they're all unavailable one day? Or if the immigrant is forced to deal with a non-Arab? Probably the biggest reason for cultivating friendships with Americans is modeling. No, not the runway sort. The kind you learned about in Psychology 101, where kids learn things by watching adults, "modeling" themselves after their parent or sibling, hence the name.

In addition to modeling (conscious or unconscious), the Arab might also ask his or her friend about American customs, rituals or traditions, as well as explanations of pop culture or language or even other Americans' behavior. At the same time, the Arab can teach the American many things about Arabic culture and provide lively descriptions of life back home (some people hate talking about their homeland, though). All in all, it seems as though having American friends usually makes a significant difference in the rate and depth of acculturation.

I find that having a balance of both Arab and American friends is helpful, in the case of the first generation American who's maybe never lived in a purely Arabic or purely American setting, as well as the recent immigrant who has lived in both. In both cases, one can practice one's weaker language, learn about unfamiliar customs and probably have a great time doing so.

As I've mentioned (more than once), Arabs place a great emphasis on *religion*. But hooking up with a compatible religious center isn't always as easy as opening a phone book. On one hand, many American cities are home to a number of churches and mosques, but on the other hand, many of these cities are a substantial drive from the places which some Arabs choose to call home. For example, it's very nice that Arab Americans living in Florida have eleven mosques and nine Coptic churches to choose from, but I personally know dozens of Arab families living in the Sunshine State who drive two and three hours each way to get their weekly fix—religious *and* social.

Our final topic in the discussion concerning Arabs and their struggle to assimilate would be *American culture*. Don't forget that most of the Middle East is literally a different world from what most Westerners are used to—where the recording artists are banned for nothing more than style of dancing, skimpy clothing (as in the case of Nancy Agram) or kissing someone (as in the case of Lebanese singer Elissa's "Agmal Ehsas" video) which (as Egyptian parliament has judged, anyway) might inflame the passions of Arabic men who should rather fit into what I call the *XXX Normalcy Model*, which involves the fuelling (or at least allowing) of men's natural arousal by women's covering up (meaning that intrigue and mystery count for something). Egypt has also banned a transsexual singer (Dana International) and his—uh, sorry—*her* songs from being heard in clubs and on the radio. Furthermore, 50 men were put on trial on the accusation of being gay; I'll spare you more examples of the restrictions, but I think you get the idea.

So it's safe to say that many Arabs are shocked by the freedoms that America affords her citizens. At the same time, many of them are grateful that they can explore the life that they may have only seen on TV—without getting sent to jail. A vast majority of immigrants have mixed feelings about their new home, manifested in differing manners. Take my friends Magdy and Wagdy. They grew up in the same apartment complex in Cairo. Inseparable as children, their brotherly relationship continued after they hit adulthood, prompting them to enter the same field of medicine so as to open their own clinic. Then, Magdy's family announced that they were moving to the States to seek improved medical treatment for his mother. Magdy made the decision to come with them, and Wagdy immediately declared that he would do the same. Two years later, they had passed their board exams and gotten jobs in the same hospital. Over lunch one day, they began discussing wives. Magdy wanted someone from back home, and had a girl in mind. Wagdy, on the other hand mentioned an American doctor who'd caught his eye. A year after that, they had each married the women they'd discussed. So when I met them, six years later, they were next-door neighbors with matching lawns but little else. Oh, they both considered themselves "American" and strived to fit in, but in different ways. Magdy's wife cooked Arabic dishes nightly, and was quite vocal in telling me how she hated America. When I asked why, she told me that there was so much to learn, that the people were so immoral, that the land was cursed (her flat in Cairo was under 1000 square feet, while her home in the suburbs is four times that). When I asked her if she had any American friends, she shook her head. When I tried talking to her in English, she giggled and told me—in Arabic—that she didn't know what on earth I was saying (she has sworn to never watch or listen to anything in English). When I told her that her boys (both under five) would have a hard time growing up without any knowledge of English, she said, "No, it's better this way. At least they'll never be confused about who they are." Her husband allows her these idiosyncrasies, but feels sad that his wife hates the land—and all its freedoms—that he has grown to love so much.

Crossing the fence, however, we see Wagdy living the high life—where Magdy drives a stodgy Escalade (the family-toting Cadillac), Wagdy and his bride drive matching Mercedes Kompressors; where Magdy has a hard time dragging his wife to an American restaurant, Wagdy and his wife hit trendy restaurants four or five times a week. Wagdy's circle of friends includes Egyptians, other Arabs, Americans, Asians, Europeans and more. His wife has improved both his English and her Arabic.

Which of these families is better off? No one can conclusively say, although I think that Magdy's wife is missing out on a lot, and keeping her children—and husband—from enjoying what could be a greatly enriched life.

Factors Affecting Acculturation

Among the factors that can affect an Arab's acculturation into America are the circumstances surrounding their old life (and their degree of choice in the decision to move), their extent of having been established in their old life, whether they came alone, and the permanence of their relocation.

In terms of the circumstances surrounding their old life, some people were miserable in the Middle East, whether for political, religious or financial issues. To them, America might seem like a haven, where they can escape pressures, restrictions, and discriminations. In terms of their choosing to move, some people are forced to leave, because of their religion or race, while others left because their land is being taken over by war. These people also might be happy to leave these horrors behind, but at the same time they may feel sadness or rage. The state of having been established can be a good thing, perhaps ensuring that the immigrant can afford to move, although, as I mentioned, being licensed (in some professions) to work in the States can take some time and thus make problems for the immigrant. On the other hand, the immigrant might hate to leave behind a thriving business or practice, for which he can't be faulted.

The presence of one's family can ease the pain of a move, although sometimes the man of the house is forced to come first, in order to save money and secure a home for his family. The presence of external controls, such as family, neighbors, or religious police, is sometimes all that stands in the way of the recent immigrant's experimentation with his new environment; for this reason, some people are actually happier to come here alone, because it means freedom, especially if no one knows who one is.

Finally, we arrive at the permanence of relocation; people who have the mentality that, "I'm in this for the long haul" end up becoming more thoroughly Americanized, in the long run. Once they think, "This is my new home, and, as much as I love the old country, I may never see it again," they're forced into acculturation, whereas someone who may or may not stay, such as visiting students, people who are up for Green Cards and people who have won a Green Card by chance (in a lottery) can sometimes acculturate just enough to work, but in terms of child-rearing and work ethic, they'll change minimally over a longer period of time. Many ill or older people realize that their time is near and only assimilate because they don't feel that they'll be able to return.

Behavioral patterns

Many people have studied the acculturation process in new Americans. Milton Gordon of the Sociology Department at the University of Massachusetts stated that for an immigrant to properly assimilate, he or she must grant *legitimacy* to other immigrant groups, display *competence* in terms of working, *civic responsibility* by being a neighbor to everyone, and, most importantly *identify themselves as Americans*, making "American" their master status, rather than black, white, Russian, Asian or whatever.

Berry, as we've mentioned, identified four styles of acculturation: *Assimilation*, or the shedding of skin, the forgetting of one's old system and full immersion into the new; *Separation*, the reverse, when the immigrant shuns the new customs in favor of the previous system; *Marginalization*, the rejecting of both old and new; and finally *Integration* (this one gets my vote for "healthiest"), or the blending of one's new culture with one's previous culture.

Finally, I've come up with my own models, based upon years of observation. The *Sybil Model* is named after the famous case concerning a woman plagued by more than one identity. While Arabs aren't all patients suffering from multiple-personality disorder, they *are* forced to separate their Arabic selves from their American selves when put in contact with Americans. The *Sybil Model* reveals a total split of identity in terms of behavior—the whole "when in Rome" mentality; when with Americans, the Arabs act as American as possible, and when with other Arabs, they behave in their normal Arab fashion. While this may seem obvious to some, it would behoove the reader to consider the fact that American/Western identity is so far removed from Eastern identity that it really is a feat to make such a seamless transition. The object may fitting in everywhere, but may also stem from a desire to keep things simple. My friend Mourad is a great example of this. When he's with Americans, one wouldn't have any idea that he's an Arab—his accent in English is flawless, and he never mentions home, family, or anything to do with his past life in Cairo. When with Egyptians, though, the twenty-one year old goes on about his plans to be a doctor, to marry a good Egyptian girl with even better morals, and the like. Since I've spent time with him in both Egyptian and American audiences, I can tell you how different the two Mourads are.

The polar opposite of the *Sybil Model* is the aptly named *Reverse-Sybil Model*, by which the subject acts totally Arabic with non-Arabs and totally Western with Arabs (like another friend, Sayed, who insists on showing off how "Arabic" he is with non-Arabs, by blaring Kazem el Saher and bringing grape leaves to work with him). When in the company of Arabs, however, Sayed behaves like the quintessential "player" (in terms of dating), listening to American rap music and eating "gourmet" and Italian food (how this makes him the "ultimate American," I have no clue, but anyway). This behavior (in general, not just Sayed's) more readily lends itself to psychoanalysis, because the observer might come up with a number of theories—such as the need to be different and/or stand out, the desire to be more of what the subjects feel they lack, even a desire for escapism, however short-lived.

At any rate, the leaving behind of any former life, whether happily or reluctantly—and regardless of current outlook, new beginnings or hope for the future—should be treated as a death and mourned accordingly. But the immigrant would do well to treasure the memory of his or her homeland, keeping the immortal words of *Tuesdays with Morrie* inspiration Morris Schwartz in mind: "Death ends a *life*, not a relationship."

11

Snapshots of Biculturalism

As previously mentioned, we're going to get acquainted with yet more Arab Americans—this time in terms of their lives in North America, beginning with non-immigrants, then moving on to every other scenario.

Americanized Non-Americans

26-year old *Samy*, a native of El Menya (who's never left the country), is a typical modern Egyptian (or so he claims). He lives with his father, goes to church, and has a job that pays for his Internet usage and mobile phone. While he's never had an out-and-out girlfriend, he's friendly with a number of young ladies in his town, occasionally taking one or another to the local nightclub. He smokes a lot, drinks a bit less, and wishes he could come to America, despite being very happy where he is. Unfortunately, his requests for clearance have never been granted by the U.S. government.

Abdo, an up-and-coming DJ and remix artist, also hails from Egypt, though he lives in Alexandria. His life almost mirrors Samy's, apart from the fact that Abdo (who doesn't drink or smoke at all) is a Moslem, lives with his mother, and has a girlfriend whom he would like to marry. Also, Abdo's been out of the country and on a number of talk shows because of his job. He has no desire to come to America, since he's happy where he is.

Sometime Sojourners

Mahmoud, whom I met in college, had come to America for educational purposes, but planned to return to his home in Dubai soon after completing his studies. Mahmoud surprised me from the start—seeking my friendship out (the whole male-female thing), tolerating my very different religious beliefs (I'm Christian and he's Moslem), and going out of his way to help me on more than one occasion (no surprise there). He was also very different than many other Middle Easterners that I'd met in that he really liked America, and agreed with many American ideals, such as equality, religious freedom, and the freedoms of speech and press. A few years later and across the state, oddly enough, I ran into yet another guy from Dubai, *Ahmed*, who shared similar ideals. Like Mahmoud, though, Ahmed was only staying long enough to obtain his degree.

I also met *Waguid* during college, although he was from the Emirates. Enrolled in flight school, he hoped to return to his home as soon as possible. He missed his family and worried about his businesses, which were located in France and throughout the Middle East. He never said anything bad about America or Americans, but I could tell how baffled he was about American customs and practices, especially nightclubs (why mingle with strangers when one could be with friends? he reasoned), nursing homes (how could anyone allow his parents to be cared for by strangers? he wondered), and credit cards (how could someone spend so much money that wasn't even his? he pondered). He's back home now, though, and probably never learned the answers to his questions.

O, Canada

Palestinian-born *Khaled*, 37, now a resident of Canada, believes that he will never set foot in America. Not because he doesn't want to—because he does. A lot. Rather, it's because he's been mistaken for a "terrorist" one time too many (he's tall and powerfully built, with hair like coal, and heavy brows and moustache to match). He states that Americans mean "What kind of foreigner are you?" when they ask "Where are you from?" whereas Canadians mean "Are you from Ottawa or Toronto or Prince Edward Island?" Having been evicted from his home in Ramallah many years ago (he refuses to speak of it, although he's mentioned, in passing, an unwillingness to ever visit the Middle East again), and having lost more than one family member to the volatile situation in his homeland, Khaled's fondest wish is to start his own family, although his search for the perfect woman was hindered when he found out that the woman he had asked to marry had some Jewish blood (he refuses to speak to Jews). So on one hand, he's closed the door to his past by becoming an easy-going, open-minded ultra-Canadian. On the other hand, his unpleasant memories keep him from associating with Jews, Americans, and anyone in uniform, tingeing every waking moment with the bitter taste of hate.

Adel is another individual who takes his now-Canadian nationalism a bit too far (in my opinion), shunning Arabs and Egyptians alike (he was born in Alexandria during the late 60s). He's also shunned his language (and denied his children the chance to learn Arabic), his heritage (his Canadian wife had no idea that he was Egyptian—she figured his dark good looks made him part Italian), his religion (he was born Coptic Orthodox but now attends a Protestant church) and his family (apart from the yearly Easter card).

Then there is Syrian-born *Maher Arar*, now a Canadian citizen, who underwent a harrowing ordeal (and has made dozens of headlines since his saga began in 2002) when United States immigration officials picked him up. We'll look at his entire story in chapter 13, but if you can't wait that long to find out what happened to him, then the short form is that he was imprisoned in a Syrian jail for over a year. His "crime?" Having been acquainted with a man who was suspected of being part of Al-Qaeda.

American-Born Arabs

Kicking off this section, we meet *Osama*, a Northerner who's only been to Egypt once. 24-year old Osama is opinionated and educated, and he shares a house with an American roommate, about 10 hours away from his parents. On one hand, Osama is mega-Egyptian: He subscribes to the same prejudices that most Arabs hold, and he wants to marry a thin, respectable girl who's never been engaged. On the other hand, he hates the Arabic language and refuses to speak it (although he understands it very well) and frowns upon many Arabic tendencies, such as drama and indecisiveness (there are a lot of Egyptian guys like Osama).

Ansaf's boys are both fine Southern gentlemen: Thirtysomething *Sobhy* is an engineer, while *Mounir*, his younger brother, is in medical school. English is the language that they speak around the house (both brothers still live at home), and American is the nationality they claim when questioned—although they *do* serve in their local Coptic Orthodox church. Apart from that, though, they don't identify with Egyptian life at all.

Eddie is a young lawyer in his late twenties. He lives in one of the largest cities in America, although his family comes from the largest city in Egypt. He's never visited Cairo, however, and doesn't speak or understand Arabic in the least. He's married to an American girl who offered to learn to cook Egyptian dishes, though he declined, since he'd never really eaten any Arabic food growing up (I know, I don't get it, either). On the other hand, he has a real hunger to meet immigrant Egyptians, stating that he would rather hear about his culture from people who have lived it, than try new foods, new customs and a new language on the eve of his thirtieth year.

Moosa's parents left Saudi Arabia and moved to America's West Coast shortly after his birth. While he speaks and understands Saudi Arabic, he has a hard time with extensive conversations in the dialect. While he enjoys the occasional Arabic film or record, he finds himself relying on translations to understand them. While his parents have a happy marriage and hope that he will marry a nice, respectable girl from a good Saudi family, Moosa has actually had a number of relationships with American women—whom he finds he can relate to much better than Arab women. Additionally, he doesn't mind if the girl he marries has had boyfriends before, and he's not hung up on finding the daughters of the most respectable families out there.

Annas is a 27-year old Syrian-American, but he's never visited Syria. Having lived his life up North, he comes across as a classy guy from Philly, but once I spoke to him, I found that his Arabic is the best I've ever heard on a non-immigrant Arab, and that he's just as respectable as any Syrian guy who's moved here. He listens to mostly Arabic music, he lives on a diet of Arabic food at home, and his parents will only allow Arabic to be spoken in the house, where he and his seven siblings still live.

Amy is a teenager who was born in America to Egyptian parents. She's the oldest of five children, all of whom understand Arabic perfectly, although Amy's a bit on the shy side when it comes to speaking. Her parents are (almost) fully Americanized, though they hold Amy and the other four to Egyptian ideals, such as respectability, thus keeping her from dating, concerts, and visiting people's homes. Amy's parents (both physicians), in true Egyptian fashion (the only one they still hold to) have forbidden the multi-talented Amy from a career in anything other than medicine—but especially not art, which, sadly, is her greatest talent. Unbeknownst to them, she has the occasional private art lesson from a French-Lebanese friend of the family who comes over on weekends.

Soher, a brilliant professor in her early thirties, is Egyptian-American. Even though she's spent a few months of every year in Egypt (since birth), she feels it wasn't enough to give her a sense of her people, who they were, and how they lived. She doesn't plan on repeating the "mistake" once she starts her own family, however. Instead, her plans include raising the children (when asked to choose between "American" or "Egyptian") as "more Egyptian" or offering them a greater range of experiences. This is how she put it: "I'd have them spend more time in Egypt (attend school there for a few years, maybe), spend time around Orthodox and Western Coptic peoples, be familiar with both the Orthodox church and Western Egyptian church, with both village life and city life in Egypt, and grow up in a multicultural setting that includes Egyptian-Americans like themselves. The natural force of the West is so strong that one needs to work harder to imbue oneself—or one's child—with the Eastern side; then a better balance can be achieved. Egyptian culture is an example of an ancient culture that has been repeatedly invaded throughout the millennia, yet we have retained an essential core of ourselves, whereas Western culture absorbs from all sources and consciously and endlessly bastardizes and then appropriates non-Western material culture or religious systems." *Ya habibti ya Soher*!

Not Just Arabic…

Here we meet two young men in very similar circumstances, but with very different approaches to being half-Lebanese.

Twenty-nine year old *Wael* is half Italian. He grew up in Beirut, but moved to Texas after high school. Even though he never left his Italian mother's side for a moment while growing up, he never made an effort to learn her language, and the only Italian food he's ever had was at the Olive Garden. Instead, he threw himself into being an Arab, even when he moved to the States. He insisted on a Lebanese bride whom he brought to Texas, and never even held her hand until they were married.

At the other end of the spectrum, we run into *Wesam*, an 18-year-old who goes by "Sam" rather than admitting to having any Arabic ties. His American mother, who was in the military before marrying Sam's father, regularly makes fun of Arabs and Arab culture. As a result, Sam's father tries too hard to be American, and his children don't know the first thing about Arabic. Sam and his younger brothers (the youngest is 16) all have girlfriends, whom they claim to have had physical contact with (their mother thinks it's cute and encourages it, even financing a hotel room for Sam's senior prom).

Recent Immigrants

Angel and her husband moved to the States a few years back, but they're anything but American. Oh, they *call* themselves American, denying their children the heritage that they were torn from, forbidding Arabic in the home and only serving American dishes like cheeseburgers and apple pie and macaroni and cheese (this apparently makes anyone an American). They persist, however, in going on about how much America is "*il balad il wiskha*," ("the filthy land") how Americans are "heartless," how the U.S. government is corrupt (never mind the fact that they come from Egypt, where a dollar or two U.S. can bribe a cop or government official), and how they wish they were back home. While continuing to serve, by the way, cheeseburgers, apple pie and Kraft Cheese and Macaroni.

We've already met Drs. *Maha* and *Botros*, who've taken on the U.S. Medical Licensing Exam, English lessons and 40-hour work weeks (all at once) since moving to Atlanta a year ago. The difference between them and Angel is that these two never say a negative word about America, and, instead, focus on the positive things their new home has afforded them, such as religious freedom (their church in the Saiid was bombed), financial opportunity, and prosperity if they worked at it. In much the same situation are fellow Copts *Makari* and his wife, *Ibtihag*, only this couple are pharmacists in their late 50s and elected to skip the licensure and go straight for opening a chain of pharmacies here, much like the seven they owned around Egypt. Drs. Makari and Ibtihag were very well-off, by any standards, and only moved here when they witnessed the death of a close friend, who made the mistake of catching a Molotov cocktail.

Not-So-Recent Immigrants

Karolina holds a prestigious governmental job in a big city. She came here from Cairo in her late teens, just after having gotten married. That was more than 30 years ago. A slight hint of accent is all that identifies her as an Arab, these days. She claims hatred for Egypt and for the oppression that she, the daughter of a Coptic Orthodox priest, suffered during her life there. She's raised her children, two boys and two girls—all in or finished with college—as Americans, to the point that they don't speak or understand Arabic. She and her family attend the occasional church service when everyone's schedule is clear. Her family is lovely, but everyone seems to be going in a different direction. She tells me that the last time they ate dinner at the dinner table was the mid-'90s.

Farid is a surgeon from Alexandria who began practicing at the age of 21. He came over in the '60s, obtaining additional education in Europe before moving to the States and completing his training up North. An entrepreneur from the start, his first investment was a hospital, after which he started buying businesses left and right. When I asked him what he loved best about his home of 30-plus years, this is what he said: "I like the freedom—freedom of expression and the way that Americans don't have to fear any government action, no matter what they say. They can produce and innovate to their hearts' content, and be rewarded for their efforts—I can't tell you how many more opportunities there are for hard-working people here! Americans also enjoy freedom of religion, which was very important to me. Another thing—the technological advances in

America are wonderful and widely available. People have a good standard of living here, and hard working people can achieve their dreams. On the other hand though, there are some bad things about America—most importantly, the moral code; there is a real moral decline in the nation, especially in the past 50 years. Television and films propagate this decline, causing many problems with the family unit.

"Having lived here for so long, I can't imagine moving back to Egypt, although I visit at least once a year. I raised my children based upon the moral standards that I grew up with. At the same time, however, I enjoy the freedoms that this country affords me, and I always tell my kids to be grateful. I enjoy living here, I vote and take my civic duties very seriously, but I never forget my homeland. I'm proud of my heritage and the way that I was brought up, I maintain my culture and language, and I'm glad to have brought my children up in the Egyptian way, glad that I taught them Arabic. I consider myself an American of Egyptian descent. Egyptian because I can never forget my roots, but American because my life has taken off from living here and the opportunities that come with that."

Rafeek, a Copt who came over at roughly the same time as Farid, has also made a success of his life in America. A gifted neurosurgeon who was denied more than one top position because of his irrepressible Christianity, he founded and now serves as the CEO of a national medical organization, where he gets to work closely with government agencies (which never would have happened back home!).

Recently voted Mother of the Year by friends and family, *Sherihan* says "I don't like America's morals, and swore to never let them infect my children. I don't like their music, their lack of respect, their manner of child-rearing; that's one thing I've noticed—Americans are very clever in bringing their children up to be self-sufficient, and that's great, but I think that this self-sufficiency is only prevalent because the parents want to lead their own lives, which I think is selfish. It's great if people grow and learn things, but it should be for the right reason!"

Finally, we meet *Dr. Sherif,* who only came to America in his late thirties and has recently celebrated his fiftieth birthday. In him, we find a man who pulled the most drastic turnaround I've ever seen—a married engineer in Cairo, he magnanimously moved to the States so that the wife who wanted to leave him (she didn't want children and he did) wouldn't be disgraced. After the divorce went through, he took up drinking, gave up smoking, and earned a medical degree. While he has the occasional "getting-to-know you" date, Sherif's actually on the prowl, looking for a new wife. The reason? He wants to adopt children (between the time I finished this book—December 2003—and this printing—June 2004, Dr. Sherif's gotten married; and his wife? She's an Egyptian and has six months to go before their first child is due).

The Younger Set

Abe is a 29-year-old Copt who owns four gas stations. He also speaks fluent "ghetto slang" and English. He has dates for every night of the week, and a personal ad on a dozen websites. He moved to America only two years ago.

Dr. Ashraf is an OB/GYN professor who just turned 30. He moved here for high school and wants to get married, now that he's through with school and has a job. He's not looking for a virgin, though—he knows all too well about the trickery that some Egyptian girls can pull, and instead wants someone that he can have fun with—before and after the wedding. He owns two new BMWs.

Ahmed, a native of Jordan, moved to the States six years ago. Even before he moved, he had some desires that couldn't be quenched in the strict and regimented Middle East. Now, however, he lives in California and regularly teaches his American friends a thing or two about the word "weird."

12

The New Generation—When Being Arab American Is All You Know

There are a number of things that can take a moment and end up haunting your entire life—speeding (points on your license are never fun), one night stands (apart from probable heartbreak or regret later on, there's always the chance of pregnancy or sexually transmitted disease), making a late payment on a bank card ("not having time to drop the bill off" could cost you seven years of spotless credit). Oh, and being torn between Eastern and Western culture (don't ask me how this only takes a moment—the lifelong haunting is enough, no matter *how* long it took!).

As I mentioned in the preface (which you should go back and read if you haven't!), I am an American; born, raised, and educated in the great Land of Opportunity, I have spent my entire residency here, save for the odd trip back to Egypt. So "of Egyptian extraction" would technically be the best way to label me, even though Americans always considered me foreign. "We" was traded for "you guys" as soon as American friends heard that I could answer the phone with alacrity in another language. In fact, the only people who counted me as an "American" were the Egyptians I had, at one point, envied so much. After all, *they* had lived in the country that I *should* have; they were the *real* Egyptians, while I was displaced. Shortchanged. Excluded from the title that should have been mine and torn from the land I'd loved since childhood.

So who was right? And, more importantly, what *was* I? After all, I had grown up in America, and missed out on all of the current things, the trends, even the new slang that had arisen since my parents' emigration. The Egypt I knew was a stranger to Egyptians of my age (which explains why all of my friends are in their forties and fifties). By the same token, I had missed out on a good number of American pastimes, as well, by virtue of having a family who drew its morals and

106

practices from the land they'd left more than twenty years ago. So while it hurt to be called "foreigner" by Egyptians, it was America that I lived in, America that had raised me and educated and *made* me. Still, to most Americans, the validity of *my* being an American was almost always in question.

From Insouciance to Fascination, and Back Again

I can't tell you how many times I've met Americans who were kind and warm and friendly to me—until they heard I was Egyptian. All at once, it would be as if I didn't speak their language; they would either stare right through me or drop their gaze, stammering and making an excuse to cut the conversation short. Or they would stay and coo over everything I said, as though I was a child just learning to speak. I wouldn't even mention this if I hadn't heard so many similar complaints from other first-generation Americans, so away we go.

A few weeks ago, Tina, who's half-Turkish and half-Iraqi, regaled me with tale after tale that could have been taken from my own life. "The other day I met this guy," she started, a gleam twinkling in her eye (meeting a guy wasn't the part that could've been taken from my own life, by the way). "He was really fine, so I threw a little smile over to him. He came over, big surprise, and started in on some line about how cute I am, which is true," she said, laughing with me. "Anyway, while he was muddling through the "Let's skip dinner and hit my place" routine, he saw a Mashallah on my bracelet and totally changed. "Wow, are you Turkish or Arab or something?" he asked, and I told him what my parents were, and how I'd been born here. Do you know what he did, Sally?"

I bit my lip on a laugh because I knew the direction the tale would take. "'Can I take you for burgers one day? Or maybe a beer? You don't have cheeseburgers in Turkey, do you?' Apparently, he forgot the part where I told him I was BORN HERE and went with his little tour-guide act. I'm kind of sorry, really, I wouldn't have minded going back to his place…oops, sorry. Too much info, eh?"

Just in case I forgot to mention it, Tina is completely Americanized, from wardrobe to dating to language—she only understands English and has never been to either parents' nation of origin.

Another thing I've noticed between Americans and first-generation ones is that if the first-generation American laughs uproariously about something, the true American will look at the first-gen like he or she is mad (strangely enough, if an immigrant were to do this, the American would think, "Oh, how cute," or "I'll bet they don't know what they're laughing at!"). This also applies to times when the first-gen is very wrapped up in telling a dramatic story—the American's expression grows all shades of the color "I have to go now" or "You're *really* scaring me." Interestingly enough, I recently witnessed this very thing between some recent immigrants and second-gens when I visited a Palestinian church one day. Oddly enough, the parties who were searching for an escape hatch were the *immigrants*, not the second-gens. So while I'm not making any formal assertions as to what makes which people laugh, I *can* inform you about the time that I was in a class taught by a foreign lady—and how the only people laughing (genuinely) at her jokes (all of them) were the five "foreign" kids in class, including me and two other first-gens.

Being the philosophical kind of gal that I am (even though I failed to come up with a valid theory about the humor thing), I came up with the theory that the Americans who were behaving xenophobically would have to go back to treating me as well as they had before—if, and only if, I acted like a total American (or, at least, *totally* dropped any talk of travel, language, etc.). The first time I tested my hypothesis was with Mandy and John, an American couple who'd appeared at my house one day, bearing invitations to their church's Monday Night Singles group (the reason a church would send a married couple to invite someone to a singles group eluded me, and so did the reason that they assumed I was single). At any rate, Mandy did all the talking, and John sat stoically on my new cut-velvet sofa. "Wow! Did you do all those yourself?" she asked, eyes bright and admiring. "I certainly did," I remarked, glad when she asked me the history of each painting and photograph (who *doesn't* love talking about their own artwork?). "Well, that guy over there is one of my best friends. Yeah, he's been in Cosmo a few times. Her? No, she's actually a med-school student in St. Louis now. Yeah, I was pretty bummed when I painted that. Ha ha."

Mandy kept looking more and more impressed, even asking to see my portfolio, but I felt bad for John, who very obviously wanted to die. So I tried to help—"I would hate to keep you guys from your other stops this evening, but maybe—if you *promise* to bring more snapshots of those dear little kids of yours—you'd like to come back sometime, Mandy? Poor John looks like he can't wait to hit the sack." Mandy burst into laughter, and John gave his first genuine smile of the evening. "Truer words were never spoken, Miss Sally. I've had a long day on the field—one of our men quit unexpectedly. So if you'll forgive me for being less than a gracious guest..."

"Not at all, my friend! Can I get either of you something? Cookies? Mango Juice? Please, at least let me get you some water," I said (entertaining is my favorite thing in the world, so I was more than a little annoyed that no one wanted a four-course dinner). When I came back with two bottles of Evian, John was staring fixedly at the Cleopatra papyrus hanging across from the kitchen. "Have you been to Egypt?" he asked, more awake than I had seen him in the past half hour. I smiled briefly and launched into my "Well, I was born *here*..." speech. His eyes sparkled as he asked me about my travels, about grape leaves and tabbouleh, about the languages I knew. I failed to notice that Mandy had begun to look as though *she* wanted to die, and stepped in again. "Er, um, yeah, those are the Lebanese and Syrians that use that phrase, actually. Yeah. You said that you guys were asleep on your feet, eh? Well, I don't wanna keep you, so..."

John shook my hand again and hoisted the grocery bag with pita bread and hummus and baklava. "Thanks again, Miss Sally. Look forward to seeing you on Monday night '*inshallah*,'" he said, chortling at his accomplishment. Mandy gave me a perfunctory hug and turned to leave. "You know, I would love to take a family portrait for you guys," I began, searching for topics that would dispel her xenophobia. She gave a halfhearted nod. "Mmm, yeah, I'll call you sometime," she tossed out before turning away. "Don't forget to bring your photo album Monday night," I said, in a last attempt. She did an about-face and grinned full force. "Of course not! And you bring your portfolio!" I was engulfed in yet another hug before she left, half turning around to wave and ask, "Mmm, is that Emporio Armani you're wearing?"

I Wouldn't Have Noticed These Unless...

There are things that would probably never have occurred to me unless I were in the unique position of being an Egyptian American, or an American Egyptian. Like the fact that some Arabic words sound a lot like curses in the English language (sorry, I can't print them here). Or like the fact that some words in English sound a lot like their translation in Arabic—and vice versa.

I've also always wondered what caused Islamic and Orthodox women alike to cover their hair (Moslems are supposed to always wear *higab*, whereas Orthodox have to cover their hair in church) when, as we've covered, their religions have more disparities than parallels (Arabic men, however, seem to be linked in the fact that long, lustrous tresses can distract them from prayer, although religious texts don't put it quite that way—rather, they say that the reason is "modesty" and "covering one's crowning glory.").

Another thing that always made me wonder was the way Middle Eastern women, who, by all accounts, are much more repressed and oppressed than the American woman, can get away with wearing so much more makeup than American women do. In fact, a number of my American friends have looked at photos of such female recording artists as Elissa, Nawal al Zoghby and Haifa Wahbi (all Lebanese, by the way, though Dalida and Fayza Ahmed aren't entirely blameless when it comes to makeup) and wondered how the women (Arabic, no less!) could get away with looking like "streetwalkers," as one guy put it. At the same time, these same repressed women who may just have arrived from the Middle East ask me why American women—nationals of the arguably richest nation on the planet—can leave their house *sans* makeup and in anything less than three-inch heels.

Finally, the absence of personal space (which I can say definitely about Egypt, and maybe some of the other Arab countries, though not all of them) in a country that's so anti-touchy-feely is another thing that always eluded me. A few Arabs might dispute this, but what I've noticed about Middle Easterners who walk together—both men and women (mostly Egyptian but also Lebanese, Moroccan, Palestinian, Syrian, Jordanian and Saudi)—is that oftentimes, one or both parties will walk with their arms, shoulders or sides touching. I used to think that this habit was found only in women, but more often than not, men do this, also. Americans who notice this (especially when it happens to them) look askance, as though the Arab's up to something funny or whatever, but it's more a cultural thing. A "You're with me" thing.

I was alerted to this fact many years ago—in grade school, actually—when I and a half-Syrian friend of mine were walking to recess. "Sally, are you okay? I mean, are you going to have a stroke?" she asked, with a perfectly straight face. I was horrified and asked her why she thought I might. "Well, it's just that you're always bumping into me. I thought you might be off balance..." she finished. I can't remember how I responded, but I'm sure it was witty. Years later, I was walking with an Egyptian friend of mine who was here on a visit. She was holding a tureen of some concoction, and I was carrying her daughter. We kept bumping arms in that patently Arabic way, when one bump jostled her daughter into my jaw. "Sorry," I gasped, surprised at how sturdy the toddler was (my jaw was certainly surprised), but my friend said "Why are you apologizing? *Ehna mashyiin maa baaad, mish kidda?*" (which means "We're walking together, aren't we?")

Things That Have Amused Me to No End

One of the most hilarious practices I've witnessed is the changing of accent before my very eyes. Westerners might not get what I mean, but Arab Americans the world over will crack a smile when they think of all the times they've witnessed "the change," too. Here's an example for the uninitiated out there: Once upon a time, I was in church (a huge Coptic Orthodox church, actually). It was the Christmas service, and Youssef, one of the younger mega-American deacons and brother to a dear friend of mine, was responsible for a reading in English. My ears perked up in anticipation of his Texas drawl. Instead, however, came this totally unfamiliar Arabic-tinged twang that must have arrived from the sky—I'd certainly never heard it before, and I saw him every week! When the after-church hullabaloo had died down about eight hours later, he came over to say hello. "So, how did I do? Did I look ok up there? Did I sound ok? Did you like what I said? Gosh, I don't even remember what I said!" I squelched the hearty laugh that was working its way into my throat (mostly because he had been *reading*, not making an acceptance speech) but nodded quickly. "You were great, tiger, but…were you nervous in any way?" His heavy brows lifted. "Yes! I was sweating buckets! What happened to the usual 20 people who attend? Did they each bring an entire family or what?" I smiled over to him and clapped him on the back, intending to leave. His naughty cousin Fadl sailed over just then, though, playing a snippet of the service on his video camera. Youssef was downing a Yoohoo—very quickly—and only half listening to the replay of the words he'd said only hours before. "Who's *that* guy? I don't remember him," he murmured, totally serious. "And what the *trash* is going on with that mega-weird accent of his?!"

Another Egyptian American girl who surrounds herself with Indians sometimes slips into a Bombay inflection when speaking to them. Or when she's stressed. A Saudi American guy I know alternates between a slight Brooklyn accent and a faint British one. My guess is that they picked up the accent that their parents are striving to have, and end up using them when they're nervous or "*mi'tenshineen*," as my friends might say.

Another odd phenomena that I've found in Arabs all over America is their penchant for speaking "ghetto." The whole "whassssup?!" thing. MTV-talk, Ebonics or just "slang," young Arabs and Arab Americans seem obsessed with hip-hop culture, especially speech-wise (and wardrobe-wise). If you don't believe me, sign on to AOL and hit "profiles" and do a search on "Egyptian" or "Lebanese" or "Arab" and you'll find more "Holla back atcha GIRLZ" and "It's all about PALESTINE BAYBAY!!!"s than you will know what to do with.

A final thing that I've noticed in regard to Arabic first-generation Americans is their annoyance with recent immigrants who make a concerted effort to "Americanize," in areas including (but not limited to) accent, slang, the blatant use of "gonna" and "wanna" (as well as other, equally irritating fake contractions), and the indefatigable optimistic nationalism that they sometimes display. This could be for two reasons—either they could be annoyed that a newbie's trying to horn in on the glory of the nation that *they*, the first-gen, grew up in, or it could be because they see this new person as a personification of the land that they weren't able to grow up in. Or it could be because they think that modern talk in a heavy accent from someone older than they are sounds *really* silly.

Traitorous First-Gens?

Some immigrant parents of American-born children are sometimes of the opinion that their children are disloyal to them and the family, by virtue of the young American's honesty. This isn't to say that Arabs are liars, but if you'll recall, image is everything. For example, an American can admit how poor her family was, or how modest his beginnings were, but not Arabs (especially Egyptians). Rather, the Arab might, well, fudge the truth a bit in order to look better—or at least not so bad. That's why you can meet 20 different Arabs from the same town who claim to have had "the most famous priest" for their father, or the "most successful pharmacist" as their mom. And Mom and Pops *were* the most famous or successful. In Junior's eyes, anyway.

Another thing that might seem disloyal to Arab parents is the first-generation (or beyond) American's seeming disloyalty to the memory of a family member who's passed on. As you may know, the standard Arab response to just having learned of someone's passing is "*il ba'aya fi hayatak*" ("may the rest be added unto your life"), or "*Allah yirhamo*," ("may God have mercy on his soul") when the name of someone who's already migrated to a different plane crops up. Many Westerners, however, rationalize that "They're in a better place now" or "Their pain has stopped" (to feel better about the fact that the anguish their loved one went through while alive is now over), or "remember the happy days" to keep their sadness at bay. To an Arab, this comes across as "They never cared!" Like the time when my mother and I were watching the Reverend Joel Osteen on TV. The Texas evangelist was speaking of his late father, saying that one should avoid despairing by dwelling on the good memories, not the loss. Mummy said "As an Egyptian, this makes me think he doesn't love his dad!" which drew a nod from me. I, a seasoned Egyptian *American*, though, saw the wisdom in Osteen's strategy, and theorized that thinking of the "good times" doesn't mean that I love that late relative any less. Of course I didn't tell *that* to Mummy.

Friendships

As we've discussed, friendships in the Arab world usually run as deep as family and require frequent conversations. Nothing wrong with that, right? Right. The only problem is that in the Old Countries, even friendship takes a back seat to family, whereas America inadvertently stresses friendship first, though many people wouldn't think that it does (if you've ever rolled your eyes to a friend or co-worker about something a relative of yours did, you're guilty!). One can find people in every assembly who see their parents once a year, if that, and call their siblings when they need something (that's not to say that this never happens with Arabs, just that it's frowned upon). In fact, an American friend of mine told me that she hadn't spoken to her sister in six years because they had nothing in common anymore. "What about blood?" I asked, incredulous. "What *about* it?" she threw back at me. "It's not enough," she finished.

Another thing that first-gens sometimes fall into is taking said friends as confidantes (rather than family), offending their parents' Arab sensibilities. I can remember a million times when I was feeling irritated or cross or just plain *sad* about something, and a well-meaning family member would ask *"Malik?"* ("what's wrong with you?") and I would say "Nothing!" They would try again (a number of times), and that was that. Until one of my best friends (for that month, anyway) called a few minutes later. I'd cast a hunted look over my shoulder and scurry to an empty room. The friend would invariably deduce that something was wrong by the tone of my voice (Egyptians are very evocative speakers) and ask what the matter was. I never volunteered anything—no, really, I didn't!—but they would usually guess that I'd had a skirmish with a professor of mine, that the cutie in my algebra class hadn't been there that day—whatever. And if they didn't guess on the first try, they would eventually get it, and I would eventually forget what had irked me to begin with. Emerging from my commandeered office, I would fail to remember that my family had known something was wrong, and go along on my merry way. Of course, I'd get stopped by the Parents Patrol, and undergo an interrogation that went something like this:

Me: "Ohh, did I drop that coffee mug? Sorry. Here, I'll get it."
Parent: "Oh, no you don't!"
Me: "Wha?!"
Parent: "Half an hour ago, *you* were seen looking ready to collapse and now everything's '*okay*?'"
Me: "Oh, that. I was just kinda annoyed."
Parent: "But you're better now?"

Me: (smiling brightly) "*Alhamdulilah*."

Parent: "You were just on the phone…"

Me: "Um…yeah. Matty's been having some trouble with this *trellis* in the—"

Parent: "So you could tell your deep, dark secrets to a stranger and not your family? What is this?"

Me: "I didn't say anything! I was just informing Matty about this new song I heard at—"

Parent: "I thought you were discussing home improvement."

Me: "When did I say that?"

Parent: "You said the word 'trellis.' You distinctly mentioned a *trellis*. Now what has that got to do with the price of tea in C—"

Me: "Ok, ok!"

Parent: "What?"

Me: "Ok, so I discussed what was troubling me with a friend."

Parent: "Ok, that's all I wanted to know. Glad you're better…"

Me: "Thanks…(smile) me, too. How're you?"

Parent: "Lousy…"

Me: "Why?! Are you ok?!"

Parent: "No…" (sad shake of the head, tragic air about them…)

Me: "What's wrong?! Tell me now!"

Parent: "My daughter has a secret life—and discusses it with STRANG-ERS!!"

Other Relationships

Being seen talking with a boy is the kiss of death when dealing with Arabic parents (if you're a girl, anyway. The more Westernized ones don't care as much, if at all). Even if you're discussing a school project, even if you're about 24, it doesn't matter (even if you're *married*, in some regions! I'll never forget the Egyptian American who told me that her father shunned her for a *week* when she accepted a ride home—from her *brother*-in-law!). Speaking with any amount of familiarity (to a guy) is the "instant mark" of an immoral woman, in many of their minds. I can't tell you how many times I was discussing a PowerPoint presentation or whatever with a guy who was in my group or team—and gotten the third degree from my parents. Once, in preparation for a visit from some Egyptians who lived nearby, my dad even went through my flat and hid all of the framed photos of me and guy friends. When I informed him that everyone had already seen them (all of them included girls and couldn't possibly be immoral, to my mind!), my mom stepped in with a disgusted expression. "Why must you shame us?" she asked, as though I spent my nights working the corner of the Main Drag. I shrugged noncommittally, then tried to reinstate the photos to their rightful places. But Daddy said something that really took the cake: "Those are staying hidden. After all, how would it look if I allowed something I disapprove of to be shown? What would the neighbors think?!"

As affronted as I was then, I knew how they felt when my sister showed me a photo of her with what appeared to be a very tall, very ugly woman. "It's a female impersonator, silly," she said. I squinted and it all made sense. My next move? Yelling at her for allowing herself to appear in a photo with a guy. *Her* next move? Informing me that I'd crossed the line and *become* my parents.

13

Stereotyping, Racial Profiling and Hate Crimes

I think it's very safe to say that at least 98 percent of Americans—natural, naturalized and everything in between—were horrified to hear about the attacks that rocked the nation on September 11, 2001. While New York City—and, indeed, most of America—sought to recover from this act of hate, people forgot their petty prejudices, working together to fight the common enemy, whoever it may have been. Unfortunately, however, many Arabs and Arab Americans were errantly swept into the category of "enemy" (although, let's face it—Americans have almost always seen Arabs as either camel jockeys lost in the big city, or in the slightly less bumpkin-esque posts of taxi drivers or owners of the local gas station, or *else* Sheikhs or terrorists—basically either backwards and bumbling or conniving and harmful).

Prejudice, scapegoating and hate crimes have shot up in occurrence, not that Americans are wrong for being scared. That doesn't mean it's okay to beat someone up because of their accent or coloring, though. Neither is it okay to wear t-shirts emblazoned with "Go Home, Ragheads!" or "Arabs = The REAL Enemy."

If I think back to my childhood, I can remember two distinct phenomena that took place anytime someone learned that I was Egyptian: foreigners, people from church, and people over 30 generally ooohed and aahed, playfully envious of my luck in being connected to such a heritage, commenting on Egypt's mystical beauty, and regaling me with their travel tales. A few kids my age would ask questions about the Pyramids or inquire as to whether I'd ever met Cleopatra.

The other group, however—much smaller in size but every bit as memorable—was composed of the youngsters who paid attention to the news (while I remained oblivious to the goings-on of the "real world"). These kids would half-jokingly ask me if I was the masked individual who'd snuck a bomb into the World Trade Center (don't forget that Sept 11, 2001 *wasn't* the first attack on the Twin Towers), if it was my family who had sparked Desert Storm, if Osama bin Laden was related to me. I didn't have the foggiest notion of what had happened in New York, that Desert Storm wasn't a heavy metal band, or who Osama was, back then. Thanks to September 11, though, I'm much more aware of current events. I also hear a much greater number of ignorant and hateful comments than I did in middle school, high school and college—combined.

Like the time I went to drop some film off at the local one-hour camera center. The lady who came to collect my 400-speed Kodak was a true Southern Belle type, complete with meticulously curled tresses, huge, sparkling eyes and an accent that would have made Delta Burke (and the rest of the cast of *Designing Women*) jealous. "Well *hello* there, precious! What can I do for you?" she asked in a musical tone. I held up the film. "Are you guys still accepting film for one-hour?" I asked, a sheepish smile in place, since closing time loomed and I was *dying* to have a look at the photos from the impromptu karaoke concert that I'd been subjected to only hours before. "Anything for you, gorgeous!" she exclaimed, slapping a one-hour envelope down and beginning to fill in the area code. "Phone number? Doubles or singles? Would you care for a CD with your order, honey? Last name, sweetie?" I began spelling my name, because I knew that merely saying it wouldn't begin to give her a clue as to how she should spell it. "B, yes, as in 'boy'-I-S-H-A-I...yep, you've got it," I finished. She beamed at me and said, "Oooh, how dyou pronounce that, sugar?" and I told her: "Beh-Shyy." I wasn't sure if her fascinated expression was genuine, or a mere product of her Southern charm, but I didn't think there was any actual *harm* in telling her what sort of name it was when she asked. I was wrong, however, if the sudden narrowing of her eyes, flattening of her voice and lack of further endearment were any indication. "They'll be done in an hour," she spat out, snatching the roll from my hand and exchanging it for the receipt at the top of the envelope. I spent the next hour wandering around the store, checking out their selection of digital cameras and plotting to tell her the fantastic story of my Great Uncle Milton, who led a battalion in one of the Services during one of the wars. The plan fell flat, however, when I realized that not only would I be lowering myself and compromising my integrity by telling a falsehood (have *you* ever met an Egyptian called "Milton?"), but that I had no idea which of the Services actually *had* battalions, whatever battalions were.

I could go on and tell you dozens of other tales that had the same sort of ending, but why bother, when you or a loved one more than likely have a tale that could top one of mine? At any rate, not all of the shocking comments I've heard are to do with "you horrible Arabs." No, some of them have been "We rock" (as when a Pakistani classmate of mine said, in mid-September 2001, "Yeah! We got them, sister!" and I said, "But Malik, there were Arab and Moslem brothers who were killed! How can you be happy about that?" and he replied with, "They got what they deserved for making their home in America!" Needless to say, I didn't see him very much after that, not that I had really seen him too much before-hand. I've actually heard it through the grapevine that he now lives in—you'll never guess this—NYC) and others, strangely enough, have had to do with "res-cuing" me.

As recently as one month ago, I've had concerned male American and Euro-pean friends "warn" me about marrying Arabs. "Sally, it's not worth it to remain un-worldly for a guy who's just going to mistreat you later," one said. Another begged me to marry a non-Arab because "Arab men don't treat women right, Sally! They make you wait on them hand and foot, they make you into a veritable baby machine, and then you end up under their thumb until the day you die." An acquaintance of mine took it a step further saying, "Arabic women are proba-bly used to the way Arabic men behave, and know what to expect, so that's not a problem. What I would fear is a hidden link to terrorists. After all, they don't come home and say 'Hey honey, I hooked up with some terrorists today!'"

In addition to such remarks regarding Arabs and social aspects of life are the more than occasional bout with discrimination against Arabs in more official set-tings, such as airports, the workplace and health-related industries, despite the Department of Justice's *Federal Protections Against National Origin Discrimina-tion*, issued in April 2001, which states:

> Federal laws prohibit discrimination based on a person's national origin, race, color, religion, disability, sex and familial status. Laws prohibiting national origin discrimination make it illegal to discriminate because of a person's birthplace, ancestry, culture or language. this means people cannot be denied equal opportunity because they or their family are from another country, because they have a name or accent associated with a national origin group, because they participate in certain customs associated with a national origin group, or because they are married to, or associate with, people of a certain national origin. (found at http://www.usdoj.gov/crt/legalinfo/natorigin.pdf)

Hate Crimes

The National Criminal Justice Reference Service defines hate crime as "the vio-lence of intolerance and bigotry, intended to hurt and intimidate someone because of their race, ethnicity, national origin, religion, sexual orientation, or disability." (Community Relations Service, 2001). The 2001 FBI report on hate crime statistics cites that "during 2001, 4,367 of the single-bias incidents were victims of racial bias, 1,828 were victims of religious bias, 1,393 were victims of sexual-orientation bias, 2,098 were victims of ethnic or national origin bias." (Hate Crime Statistics, 2001 found at http://www.fbi.gov/ucr/01hate.pdf). But mere numbers won't tell us who these victims are.

The biggest targets for hate crimes these days seem to be those Arabs whose accent or coloring sets them apart from the stereotypical "White Man" (or those who merely "look Arab," even if they've never heard a word of Arabic in their life—whether because they're second, third, or tenth generation, or because they're another ethnicity altogether, one which may have nothing to do with Islam or the Middle East), those who speak about or defend Arab issues, those who display flags belonging to Middle Eastern countries, and those who don cultural or religious garb, such as the *galabaya* (long dress-like garment), the *kiffeya* (a traditional red and white checkered scarf worn around the head, what Westerners imagine Saudi sheikhs to wear, what Yasser Arafat was famous for wearing), the turban or, for women, the veil (ranging from the *higab*, which only covers the hair, to the, *burqa*, the *chador* and the *abbayah*, which cover much more).

Racial Profiling and Other Discriminatory Acts

Hate crimes aren't the only ways to hurt a person, though. Syrian-born Canadian Maher Arar found this out the hard way back in 2002, when he was detained by American officials at JFK in New York, as he was returning to Montreal after a Tunisian holiday. Let's have an abbreviated look at his case:

September 26, 2002

Arar is detained at JFK by U.S. Immigration and Naturalization officials who allege Arar has links to al-Qaeda. They detain and question him without informing Canadian officials.

October 7 or 8, 2002

Arar deported to Syria.

October 10, 2002

Canadian officials learn of Arar's deportation.

October 22, 2002

Arar's imprisonment in a Syrian prison is discovered.

October 29, 2002

Canada issues travel advisory to all Canadians born in Iran, Iraq, Libya, Sudan, or Syria to reconsider entering the United States, following a U.S. decision to photograph and fingerprint them upon entry into the U.S.

October 5, 2003

Syria finally frees Maher Arar.

Oct. 6, 2003

375 days after Maher's first arrest by U.S. immigration officials, he (finally) returns to Montreal.

Just in case you didn't notice the entry for October 29, go have another look at it. Yes, you *did* just read that correctly! All Arabs born in Iran, Iraq, Libya, the Sudan or Syria have to be photographed and fingerprinted upon entry into the United States, much like a common criminal, regardless of age or religion! It's very kind of the Canadian government to care enough to alert their citizens of this, but at the same time, it seems that in terms of the protection that it should afford citizens, a Canadian passport doesn't hold much weight anymore (in America, anyway…).

For example, Iranian-born photojournalist Zahra Kazemi, who became a Canadian citizen in 1974, died of a fractured skull while in the custody of the Iranian government after having been arrested for trying to photograph demonstrations in her home country. Another Canadian, William Sampson, was jailed in Saudi Arabia for 31 months after being accused of setting off a car bomb in Britain, where he lives. 43-year old Nguyen Thi Hiep was charged with drug trafficking and executed by a firing squad in Vietnam, even though she held a Canadian passport, and even though the Canadian government was promised that Hiep would remain alive until new evidence (which would have proved she was framed) was reviewed. Which goes to show that the wheels of justice can be headed off by hot tempers. Or racial (and adopted-nationality based) profiling.

The Patriot Act

What may have sounded like a wonderful and effective manner of bringing to light covert (and possibly illegal and/or terrorist-related) activities in late 2001 smacks of over-the-top Orwellian spying on what may just turn out to be your average Joe (or Youssef, as the case may be) in 2003. Yes, that's right. The "*Uniting and Strengthening America by Providing Appropriate Tools Required to Intercept and Obstruct Terrorism*" (U.S.A PATRIOT ACT, 2003) is not a hit anymore. People were much more eager to staunch terrorism when the threat loomed large, but now it seems that the government is going too far. Prying into the private affairs of someone named Ahmed or Abdullah or Mahmoud is perfectly acceptable, and people are happy to hear that one more person "checks out," but try hitting a non-Arab, non-Moslem, non-accented White person with it and people start making a to-do about their civil liberties being trampled upon. The Department of Justice answers questions about the Patriot Act in its page lifeandliberty.gov. But writers Dahlia Lithwick and Julia Turner, in a September 2003 article for Slate.com, inform us that U.S. Attorney General John Ashcroft has gone out on a "'*Patriot Rocks' concert tour…which has him visiting 18 cities and talking up the act to local law enforcement officials…contending that had the Patriot Act been in place earlier, 9/11 wouldn't have happened and that absent a Patriot Act, the country may have seen more 9/11s over the past two years—a double-double negative that's unprovable, but enough to scare you witless.*"

Lithwick and Turner go on to enlighten everyone who doesn't subscribe to a newspaper or own a television about the Patriot II act, which was promptly shot down, and the VICTORY act, which apparently has the same DNA as the Patriot II act, only focused on the war on drugs. Senator Orrin Hatch, John Ashcroft, and others want us to believe that these three acts (and their offspring) won't really change anything, while the ACLU wants us to believe that this violation is altering what America stands for. The "violations" include laws dealing with private records, alien detentions, new electronic surveillance, the Foreign Intelligence Surveillance Act (FISA), and "sneak and peek" warrants. Former Vice President Al Gore, in mid-November 2003, said of those who supported the aforementioned acts, "They have taken us much farther down the road toward an intrusive, 'big brother'-style government—toward the dangers prophesied by George Orwell in his book '1984'—than anyone ever thought would be possible in the United States of America." If he's in earnest, then he might turn into a political hero in the coming years, championing the privacy of the American people. On the other hand, 2004 is an election year…

So what does all of this claptrap mean, then? Slimy politicians might say "Nothing harmful," activists might say "The beginning of the end," but I have to go with "All of the above"—because while invasions of privacy are horrible things, I'm willing to bet that they've been going on for as long as the government has had the technology to do so. An American friend of mine even "informed" me (soon after the attacks in New York) that "the feds" had a tap on the phone lines of known Arab Americans, and that I should watch what I said—even jokes or off-handed comments—because they were "out for blood." While I took issue to the way he phrased it, I understood what he meant: it's all too easy for Arab American high-schoolers or college kids to say something that might be taken the wrong way (remember how effusive and dramatic some Arabs can be in their speech).

So, while I should thank my friend for the tip, I'm saddened that anyone has to be targeted, and more so for people like Maher Arar and Zahra and others like them, who had (and most likely will keep having) the misfortune to catch the eyes of people "out for blood."

So, what now? I don't think anyone (on Earth, anyway) has the answers. In terms of terrorism, I don't think that targeting Arabs (or any other race) is the way to go—what about people like Timothy McVeigh or Ted Kaczynski or even Columbine shooters Dylan Klebold and Eric Harris? They were all Americans and yet they turned on their own people.

So the business of terror, as you may have guessed, isn't monopolized by Arabs, and we should never hide who we are just because we fear repercussions that have nothing to do with us (this applies to Western readers, too. The "not hiding" bit, I mean). At any rate, I think that if each of us—where "us" means "humans"—were to forget about prejudice and stereotyping and be a friend to everyone, no matter what their nationality (real or imagined), hate crimes (all of them, not just anti-Arab) would lessen and understanding would increase. That's not too much to ask for, is it?

Epilogue: Ok Then…Now What?

So, what have we learned in the past 13 chapters? Lots of information and a bit of history, yes…

But I hope the frustration, sorrow, anxiety, and "who-am-i-ness" has come across to those who have never felt—or understood—it. I think that the first generation is the worst off, in one respect—being torn between two cultures and belonging solely to neither. But I also feel that, armed with a roadmap as to what obstacles may arise, the first-gen is in a unique position to see things that an immigrant or an American might not, to get the best of both worlds.

In terms of immigrants, I hope that what you've read—especially Section Two—may help you and your children as you seek to make a new home for yourselves.

And now—to all of my bicultural readers—I'd just like to say that I, too, have those days when I don't want to hear the Arabic language, or deal with the Arabic mentality, or even eat any pita and grape leaves. Sometimes it's just too much to deal with, and fellow Arabs don't make it any better.

But I also know that at the end of those days, I—and you—have something that's so precious, something that makes us who we are, something that we should never strive for, or try to hide. We have the language, the blood, the *heart*—and that can never be taken from us. Alhamdulilah. *Alhamdulilah…*

Glossary—Arabic

Ahlan wasahlan—"Welcome/hello."

Alhamdulilah—"Praise be to God."

Allah/Rabinah—God.

Allah yi barkak—"May God bless you."

Baba—Father, Dad.

Habibi—"Dear" or "Darling." Also *habibti* (f.).

Ha Mawitik—Literally "I will kill you"

Ha nott fi kirshik—Can be used instead of "*Ha Mawitik.*"

Haram—Religious usage—one step away from "forbidden"—i.e. "Moslems don't eat pork because it's *haram.*" Common usage—the equivalent of "come, now, have some pity." i.e.—"*Haram!* Don't kill that butterfly!"

Ha'tom ra'bitik—Can be used instead of "*Ha Mawitik.*"

Inshallah—"God willing" or "may God will it."

Khalas—Literally "It's over!" or "It's finished/ended."

Maalish—"Never mind," or "it's ok."

Rabinah maak—"God be with you."

Yalla—"Come on!"

Arabic Names

Maybe you're not up on the genders behind some of the names mentioned throughout the book. A glance here should help you realize that "Ezzat" is a man's name, and so is "Mina."

Male

Adel, Ahmed, Akram, Amir, Ashraf, Aziz, Basem, Boulos, Boutros, Elia, Ezzat, Fadel, Fady, Fahim, Farid, Fawzy, Gamal, Habib, Hakim, Hisham, Hosny, Ihab, Imad, Jafar, Kamal, Kareem, Khaled, Khalil, Khayrat, Lotfi, Malak, Malik, Mohammed, Maged, Maher, Mina, Mohsen, Mouneer, Mostafa, Mourad, Moussa, Nabeel, Nader, Nael, Nagy, Nageeb, Nayef, Nour, Omar, Osama, Qasim, Rafiq, Saleh, Salim, Sameh, Samer, Samir, Samuel, Samy, Sayed, Shafiq, Sherif, Shokri, Sobhy, Tamer, Tawfiq, Wael, Wadie, Waguid, Wasim, Wesam, Yasser, Youssef, Zaki, Zayn.

Female

Amgad, Amira, Ansaf, Asala, Ashraf (rare, but possible), Aysha, Aziza, Bassma, Dayana, Fahima, Fairuz, Fatima, Fayza, Ghada, Ghaliya, Ghufran, Habiba, Hadya, Haifa, Hakima, Hana, Hanaa, Hanan, Hiba, Houda, Ibtehag, Iman, Jehan, Khadija, Layla, Lamis, Lamya, Latifah, Lawahez, Maha, Malak, Maryam, Mareya, Mona, Nada, Nadia, Naema, Nawal, Nermine, Nour, Ranya, Rasha, Sabah, Sahar, Samia, Shakira, Sherihan, Sherine, Soher, Taliba, Warda, Widad, Youssra, Zahra.

Glossary—English

abaya, abbaya: Single piece garment placed on the head, covering the entire body, apart from the face.

acculturation: **1:** cultural modification of an individual, group, or people by adapting to or borrowing traits from another culture; *also*: a merging of cultures as a result of prolonged contact **2:** the process by which a human being acquires the culture of a particular society from infancy.

Arab: **1:** a member of the Semitic people of the Arabian peninsula **2:** a member of an Arabic-speaking people.

Arabic: **1:** a Semitic language orig. of the Arabs of the Hejaz and Nejd that is now the prevailing speech of a wide region of southwestern Asia and northern Africa **2:** of, relating to, or characteristic of Arabia or the Arabs **3:** of, relating to, or constituting Arabic.

assimilation: **1: a:** an act, process, or instance of assimilating **b:** the state of being assimilated **4:** the process of receiving new facts or of responding to new situations in conformity with what is already available to consciousness.

burqa, burga: a veil that completely hides the body and face, worn by Moslem women (especially in Afghanistan).

chador: a large cloth worn as a combination head covering, veil, and shawl usually by Muslim women (especially in Iran).

colonialism: **1:** the quality or state of being colonial **2:** something characteristic of a colony **3 a:** control by one power over a dependent area or people **b:** a policy advocating or based on such control.

culture shock: a sense of confusion and uncertainty sometimes with feelings of anxiety that may affect people exposed to an alien culture or environment without adequate preparation.

democracy: 1 a: government by the people; *especially*: rule of the majority **b:** a government in which the supreme power is vested in the people and exercised by them directly or indirectly through a system of representation usually involving periodically held free elections **2**: a political unit that has a democratic government **3** *capitalized*: the principles and policies of the Democratic party in the U.S. **4**: the common people especially when constituting the source of political authority **5**: the absence of hereditary or arbitrary class distinctions or privileges.

diaspora: 1: *capitalized* **a:** the settling of scattered colonies of Jews outside Palestine after the Babylonian exile **b:** the area outside Palestine settled by Jews **c:** the Jews living outside Palestine or modern Israel **2 a:** the breaking up and scattering of a people: MIGRATION **b:** people settled far from their ancestral homelands **c:** the place where these people live.

ethnocentric: an adjective describing the condition of viewing and judging (often in pejorative terms) other cultures and societies according to the (usually taken-for-granted) assumptions of one's own society. By way of contrast, anthropology is concerned not only to highlight our assumptions but also to show that other cultures and societies are different to our own, but not any worse or better.

Ethnic: 1: HEATHEN **2 a:** of or relating to large groups of people classed according to common racial, national, tribal, religious, linguistic, or cultural origin or background **b:** being a member of an ethnic group **c:** of, relating to, or characteristic of ethnics.

ethnic: a member of an ethnic group; *especially*: a member of a minority group who retains the customs, language, or social views of the group.

ethnocentric: characterized by or based on the attitude that one's own group is superior.

Eurocentric: centered on Europe or the Europeans; *especially*: reflecting a tendency to interpret the world in terms of western and especially European values and experiences.

Globalism: a national policy of treating the whole world as a proper sphere for political influence.

Imperialism: **1:** imperial government, authority, or system **2:** the policy, practice, or advocacy of extending the power and dominion of a nation especially by direct territorial acquisitions or by gaining indirect control over the political or economic life of other areas; *broadly:* the extension or imposition of power, authority, or influence.

Intifada: Arabic word which means a shaking off or shivering because of fear or illness. It also means abrupt and sudden waking up from sleep or unconcerned status. Politically, the word came to symbolize the Palestinian uprising against the Israeli occupation.

jihad: **1:** a holy war waged on behalf of Islam as a religious duty **2:** a crusade for a principle or belief.

modernization: **1:** the act of modernizing: the state of being modernized
2: something modernized: a modernized version.

multicultural: of, relating to, reflecting, or adapted to diverse cultures.

occupation: **1 a:** the possession, use, or settlement of land: **b:** the holding of an office or position **3 a:** the act or process of taking possession of a place or area: SEIZURE **b:** the holding and control of an area by a foreign military force **c:** the military force occupying a country or the policies carried out by it

Orientalism: **1:** a trait, custom, or habit of expression characteristic of Oriental peoples
2: scholarship or learning in oriental subjects.

race: **1:** a breeding stock of animals **2 a:** a family, tribe, people, or nation belonging to the same stock **b:** a class or kind of people unified by community of interests, habits, or characteristics **3 a:** an actually or potentially interbreeding group within a species; *also:* a taxonomic category (as a subspecies) representing such a group **b:** BREED **c:** a division of mankind possessing traits that are transmissible by descent and sufficient to characterize it as a distinct human type **5:** distinctive flavor, taste, or strength.

Rupush: a loose outer garment that flows down past the knees and covers the arms (especially in Iran).

Rusari: a large scarf that covers the hair, shoulders and neck (in Iran)

Thawb: a simple, ankle length shirt of wool or cotton. (in Saudi Arabia)

Traditional Saudi headwear: includes a *ghutra*, (large diagonally-folded cotton square) worn over a *kufiyyah* (skull cap) and held in place by an *igaal*(a double-coiled cord circlet). A flowing floor-length outer cloak, called a *bisht*, is usually made of wool or camel hair in black, beige, brown or cream.

Westernization: conversion to or adoption of western traditions or techniques

Links and Resources

Let it be said that I don't endorse or subscribe to at least half of what's written in the following websites, but they're a good starting point if you're interested in any of these topics. Also, I take no responsibility as to how reliable and/or valid these works are (as with anything on the Internet, eh?). Anyway, happy reading…

Anti-Arab and Arab discrimination cases in the news

http://www.cbc.ca/news/background/arar

http://www.freemaherarar.com

http://en2.wikipedia.org/wiki/Maher_Arar

http://www.thestar.com/NASApp/cs/ContentServer?pagename=thestar/Layout/Article_Type1&call_pageid=971358637177&c=Article&cid=1068117068855

http://www.thestar.com/NASApp/cs/ContentServer?pagename=thestar/Layout/Article_Type1&call_pageid=971358637177&c=Article&cid=1068073812382

http://en.wikipedia.org/wiki/Zahra_Kazemi

http://cnews.canoe.ca/CNEWS/Canada/2003/11/04/246859-cp.html

http://www.ccadp.org/canadavietnam.htm

http://ccadp.org/nguyencanada.htm

Arab Resources

American Arab Anti-Discrimination Committee—http://www.adc.org/

American Arab Chamber of Commerce—http://www.AmericanArab.com/

Arab American Institute—http://www.aaiusa.org/

League of Arab States—http://www.Arableagueonline.org/Arableague/index.jsp

Middle East Institute—http://www.mideasti.org/

Middle East Policy Council—http://www.mepc.org

National Council on U.S.-Arab Relations—http://www.ncusar.org/

Arab American and Chaldean Council—http://www.Arabacc.org/

Healing the Nation: The Arab American Experience After September 11—http://www.aaiusa.org/PDF/healing_the_nation.pdf

Democracy now!—http://www.democracynow.org/

Arab Culture

Arab Culture Primer—http://www.suite101.com/welcome.cfm/Arab_culture_and_identity

100 Questions and Answers about Arab Americans—http://www.freep.com/jobspage/Arabs.htm

Biculturalism and Multiculturalism

Multicultural center for Research and Practice—http://www.multiculturalcenter.org/

Cultural studies—http://www.culturalstudies.net/

Cultural pluralism—http://www.bgsu.edu/colleges/library/infosrv/lue/acs250ethnic.htm
http://www.uvm.edu/~ccpuvm/

http://prof.mt.tama.hosei.ac.jp/~hhirano/academia/leibniz.htm

Boycotting groups

The official Boycott Israel site—http://www.boycottisrael.org

The official Boycott America site—http://www.boycottAmerica.org/

Culture shock resources

Surviving Culture shock—http://www.dal.ca/~studyab/GuideForStudents/
StageTwo/stageTwo011.html

http://www.synergyorg.com/cltc%20page3.htm

Historical information

Ancient Egyptian resources—http://home.prcn.org/~sfryer/Egypt.html

Honor killings and Hymen Reconstruction

Dangers of…http://net-burst.net/singles/hymen.htm

Honor killings and…
http://www.alicemagazine.com/features/2000_01/murder_honor.html

Info about surgical procedure—http://labiadoctor.com/hymen.html

Islamic sites

Sunni beliefs—http://www.sunnah.org/

Shiite beliefs—http://www.shia.org/

http://www.islamic-paths.org/Home/English/Discover/Pillars/
Shahada_Main.htm

http://muttaqun.com/

Liberal Islamic Network—http://www.islamlib.com/page.php

TV and Sexual Content In The Light Of Islamic Morals…http://www.
blackjournalism.com/tvand.htm

Behind the Veil—http://www.utexas.edu/features/archive/2002/veil.html

Traditional Saudi dress—http://unlhrfsls.unl.edu/hrfs865/SAUDI/CLOTHING.HTM

Suffism—http://thetruth.hypermart.net/suffism.htm

http://www.al-islam.org/beliefs/spirituality/suffism.html

Hezbollah

http://www.terrorismanswers.com/groups/hezbollah_print.html

Language resources

Arabic—http://www.al-bab.com/Arab/language/lang.htm

http://www.wannalearn.com/Academic_Subjects/World_Languages/Arabic/

http://www.Arabic2000.com/Arabic/public/common.html

Arabic-English dictionary-online!—http://www.almisbar.com/dict_page.html

Palestine

A Flash timeline of Palestine's history—http://www.usatoday.com/graphics/news/gra/gisrael2/flash.htm

Financial aid to Israel—http://www.wrmea.com/html/us_aid_to_israel.htm

Intifada—http://www.intifada.com/

Ramallah online—http://www.ramallahonline.com/

Patriot Act

A guide to the Patriot Act—http://slate.msn.com/id/2087984/

ACLU's thoughts on PATRIOT…http://www.aclu.org/SafeandFree/SafeandFree.cfm?ID=13371&c=206

Section-by-section analysis of PATRIOT—http://www.publicintegrity.org/dtaweb/downloads/Story_01_020703_Doc_1.pdf

Archive of information regarding the act—http://www.epic.org/privacy/terrorism/usapatriot/

Links to the entire act—http://www.eff.org/Privacy/Surveillance/Terrorism/hr3162.php
http://www.epic.org/privacy/terrorism/hr3162.html

Racial Profiling

http://en.wikipedia.org/wiki/Racial_profiling

Religious Resources and Articles

The Kybalion—http://bobert1.home.mindspring.com/kybalion.html

Beliefnet—http://aol.beliefnet.com/

State of Assyria website—http://www.atour.com/

Maronites

http://saintjudechurch.org/images/Maronites/body_maronites.html

http://www.cin.org/bushra/mag1196/0896maro.html

Orthodox

Armenian Church—http://www.armenianchurch.org/

Syrian Orthodox Church in America—http://www.syrianorthodoxchurch.org/

Greek and Antiochian Orthodox—
http://www.unicorne.org/orthodoxy/septembre02/conversions.htm

Antiochian Orthodox Archdiocese of North America—http://www.antiochian.org/

Iraqis

http://i-cias.com/e.o/iraq_4.htm

Chaldean American Student Association—http://www.umdcasa.com/html/history/introduction.html

Chaldean Association of America—http://www.chaldeanfederation.com/

Copts

Encyclopaedia Coptica—http://www.coptic.net/

History of the Coptic Church—http://www.copts.net/history_book.htm

History of the Coptic language—http://www.stshenouda.com/coptlang/copthist.htm

More Coptic language resources—http://ourworld.compuserve.com/homepages/ekladious/Coptic.html

U.S. Copts site—http://home.netcom.com/~us_copts/copts.html

Copts.com—http://www.copts.com/

Southern U.S. Coptic Diocese—http://suscopticdiocese.org/

Coptic Orthodox Church Centre, UK—http://www.copticcentre.com/

St. Basil Liturgy—http://pharos.bu.edu/cn/prayers/StBasilLiturgy.html

Coptic Orthodox Electronic Publishing—http://www.coepaonline.org/

Religious Genocide

The Cross in the Crescent—http://www.catholic.net/rcc/Periodicals/Igpress/2002-01/dossier.html

Disappearing Christians in the Middle East, by Daniel Pipes—http://www.danielpipes.org/article/1050

Christian Persecution by Arafat, by Joseph Farah—http://www.worldnetdaily.com/news/article.asp?ARTICLE_ID=30299

Indigenous people under the rule of Islam, by Frederick P. Isaac—http://www.atour.com/religion/docs/20010803a.html

Turks are evicting native Christians—http://www.cilicia.com/armo10c-nyt19150712.html

Why America and the Middle East...

Why America is hated in the ME—http://www.globalissues.org/Geopolitics/MiddleEast/TerrorInU.S.A/Why.asp

Why did the terrorists attack? http://www.njdc.org/reports.php?show=203

Explaining Arab Anger—http://news.bbc.co.uk/1/hi/world/middle_east/1552900.stm

Why people hate America and Americans—http://www.trinicenter.com/kwame/2002/Nov/112002.htm

Love-hate between America and the ME—http://abcnews.go.com/sections/nightline/DailyNews/WTC_Arab_us_010926.html

Zionist-American plot? (MEMRI article)—http://www.memri.de/uebersetzungen_analysen/themen/usa_und_der_nahe_osten/us_initiative_III_06_01_03.html

Pat Buchanan's 'Why does Islam hate America?'
http://www.iconservative.com/why_does_islam_hate_America.htm

'Why they hate America'—http://www.unc.edu/depts/diplomat/archives_roll/2002_01-03/editor_hate/editor_hate.html

'Why many Arabs hate America'—
http://www.antiwar.com/orig/mcconnell8.html

'Why does the world hate America?' by Daniel Pipes—
http://www.danielpipes.org/article/1000

"Why does the world hate America?' by Hafiz Muhammed Ahmed—http://
johnw.host.sk/ar/why_does_the_world_hate_America.htm

Literature Review

Acho, A.—The Chaldean Link, from http://www.umdcasa.com/html/info/link.html This page features information and a chart which argue that Abraham, from Ur of the Chaldees, indirectly fathered Christianity, Islam and Judaism.

Affluenza: PBS program on the epidemic of overconsumption, from http://www.pbs.org/kcts/affluenza/ This page is the companion to a PBS special on "Affluenza," which expounds upon the diseases of materialism and overconsumption in America, including diagnosis and treatment.

Alexandria 2000. (n.d.). The history of Alexandria, Egypt, from http://www.alexsite.com/html/assort/roman.html This page tells of the Roman period in Alexandria, including a brief mention of the Coptic Church and its persecution by Diocletian.

Althen, G. (1988). American Ways: A Guide for Foreigners in the United States. Yarmouth, Maine: Intercultural Press, Inc. The introduction and Part I of this book provide unusually perceptive observations about Americans and the way they think of foreigners, as well as the ways foreigners differ from Americans.

American Civil Liberties Union. (2003, August 26). ACLU says Justice Dept.'s PATRIOT Act website creates new myths about controversial law, from http://www.aclu.org/SafeandFree/SafeandFree.cfm?ID=13371&c=206 This page cites that the Department of Justice is spreading myths about the USA PATRIOT Act, and goes about dispelling them.

Anderson, G. T., (2003, September 12). The cost of the good life—Spending on stuff seems a never-ending spiral in America; there's always something new to buy. *CNN Money*, from http://money.cnn.com/2003/09/11/pf/saving/price_of_wow/index.htm In this page, the author enlightens readers about the history of spending, as well as current and future trends.

Arab American Institute. (n.d.). Arab American Demographics, from http://www.aaiusa.org/demographics.htm This page sets forth definitions and classifications and demographics of Arab Americans, including Origins, Income and Religion.

Ashabranner, B. (1991). An Ancient Heritage: The Arab-American Minority. New York: HarperCollins, Inc. This is a children's book which offers many historical facts about First and Second Wave immigrants, as well as case studies of members belonging to both groups.

Atour: The State of Assyria. (n.d.). Religious Persecution and Ethnic Genocide of Assyrians in the Middle East, from http://www.atour.com/holocaust This page provides a wealth of knowledge about Assyrians and their trials, in the form of text and links, both internal and external.

Berry, J. W., (1980) Acculturation: theory, models and some new findings, from http://www.rrz.uni-hamburg.de/psych-3/seminar/dahme/John%20W.pdf This document sets forth the basic tenets of Berry's models of acculturation.

Buchanan, P. (n.d.). Why does Islam hate America? from http://www.iconservative.com/why_does_islam_hate_america.htm This informative article gives a well-thought out argument for leaving the Middle East to her own devices.

Bury, C., Gizbert, R. (2003, September 26). The Love-Hate Relationship—The Arab World's Mixed Feelings Over America, from http://abcnews.go.com/sections/nightline/DailyNews/WTC_Arab_us_010926.html In this article, the authors state that the Arab world does not eschew the creations of the West, and yet behaves hypocritically, especially in the face of the equality and democracy that America teaches but doesn't always practice. The authors also postulate that the Arab world's anti-American sentiments rise from Israeli support.

Canadian Coalition Against the Death Penalty. (2000, June 1). News articles, from http://www.ccadp.org/canadavietnam.htm This page recounts the plight of a wrongfully accused—and murdered—Vietnamese-Canadian.

Canadian Coalition Against the Death Penalty. (2000, June 4). Nguyen Thi Hiep, from http://ccadp.org/nguyencanada.htm This page contains updates and a timeline of the wrongfully-executed Vietnamese-Canadian.

Canadian Press. (2003, November 6). Sampson lambastes Canada over torture cases. *Toronto Star*, from http://www.thestar. com/NASApp/cs/ContentServer?pagename=thestar/Layout/ Article_Type1&call_pageid=971358637177&c=Article&cid=1068117068855 In this article, a wrongfully imprisoned Canadian citizen blames Canada for allowing him to be tortured and detained in Saudi Arabia.

Cannuyer, C. (2001). Coptic Egypt: The Christians of the Nile. New York: Harry N. Abrams, Inc. This book has many helpful explanations of the many names that Copts have been called over the years.

Chaldean Federation. (n.d.). The lessons of history and the identity of a people, from http://www.chaldeanfederation.com/chaldean-page-01.htm This page (and the two that follow) provides a brief but informative history of the Chaldean people.

CIA World Factbook (2003) from http://www.odci. gov/cia/publications/factbook/index.html This page is a gateway to the World Factbook of the CIA, which includes statistical, demographic and financial information about every country in the world.

Coming home. (n.d.), from http://www.usask.ca/nursing/International/niger/ cominghome.htm This page offers helpful advice for re-entry into one's home country, after a trip abroad.

Coptic Orthodox Church Network. (n.d.). The Coptic Calendar of Martyrs, from http://www.copticchurch.net/easter.html This document provides a history of the Coptic Church Calendar, historical trivia about the calendar, as well as the Coptic and Arabic names of each month.

Copts.com (n.d.). Coptic Demands, from http://www.copts.net/demands.asp This page lists 20 demands that Copts have put together for submission to the Egyptian Government.

Copts.com (2003). Egypt attempts to close a Coptic church, from http:// www.copts.net/detail.asp?id=451 This article tells about the 2003 attack on a Coptic church in Asyut during a service, including the trampling of the Gasad (body).

Dorland's Illustrated Medical Dictionary. (n.d.). The "H" section, from http://www.mercksource.com/pp/us/cns/ cns_hl_dorlands.jspzQzpgzEzzSzppdocszSzuszSzcommonzSzdorlandszSzdorland zSzdmd_h_18zPzhtm Provides definitions of many hymeneal procedures.

Egyptian Sourcebook for Castle Falkenstein-Alexandria. (n.d.). Alexandria, from http://cfegypt.www3.50megs.com/Alexandria/Alexandria.html A somewhat far-reaching page which not only recounts the history of Alexandria, but also mentions the best landmarks and sightseeing destinations in town.

Electronic Frontier Foundation. (2001, October 25). USA PATRIOT ACT, as passed by Congress, from http://www.eff.org/Privacy/Surveillance/Terrorism/ hr3162.php This document contains the whole of the USA PATRIOT Act.

Ethnologue.com (n.d.). ISO 639 Code: ara, from http://www. ethnologue.com/show_iso639.asp?code=ara This page explains the classifications of Modern Standard Arabic.

Farah, J. (2003, January 3). Christian Persecution by Arafat. *World Net Daily*, Article 30299, from http://www.worldnetdaily. com/news/article.asp?ARTICLE_ID=30299 This article asserts that Arafat is responsible for the persecution in and mass exodus of millions of Christian Arabs from Palestine.

Free Maher Arar. (2003, March 14). The plight of Maher Arar, from http:// www.freemaherarar.com This page sets forth a timeline of the plight of Syrian-Canadian Maher Arar.

Hate Crime Statistics. (2001). Retrieved October 1, 2003, from http:// www.fbi.gov/ucr/01hate.pdf This document gives statistics for various hate crimes.

International Student & Exchange Services, Dalhousie University. (n.d.). Cultural Adaptation, from http://www.dal.ca/~studyab/GuideForStudents/ StageTwo/stageTwo011.html This page quotes Kohls' definition of culture shock and offers assistance with its symptoms.

Khashan, H. (Winter 2001). Arab Christians as symbol. *The Middle East Forum*, 8, Article 4, from http://www.meforum.org/article/4 This article gives an excellent and complete (for its length) history of the persecution of Christian Arabs, a listing of the obstacles that Christian Arabs face, and possible solutions. Highly recommended.

Krawchuk, C. (2003, November 6). In depth: Maher Arar. CBC New, from http://www.cbc.ca/news/background/arar An overview of the plight of Maher Arar.

Lancaster, J., (1997, March 18). After Violent Attacks, Ancient Coptic Minority Fears It Has Become the Target of Islamic Militants. *Washington Post*, page A 12, from http://home.netcom.com/~us_copts/copts.html This article recounts attacks on Copts and ponders the situation.

Lithwick, D., Turner, J. (2003, September 8). A guide to the Patriot Act. *Slate Magazine*, from http://slate.msn.com/id/2087984/ An excellent article that simplifies the USA PATRIOT Act, this guide (beginning with Part I) explores the act and its many ramifications on the civil liberties of Americans. Highly recommended.

Middle East Council of Churches. (n.d.). Directory of Member Churches, from http://www.mecchurches.org/links/directory/memberc.asp This page is a directory of every church belonging to the Middle East Council of Churches.

Middle East Media Research Institute. (January 6, 2003). Arab Media Reactions to The U.S.-Middle East Partnership Initiative Part III: It's a Zionist/American Plot, from http://www.memri.de/uebersetzungen_analysen/themen/ usa_und_der_nahe_osten/us_initiative_III_06_01_03.html This article makes many valid points that Arabs have, and which are routinely misunderstood by Westerners. Highly recommended.

Nydell, M. K. (2002). Understanding Arabs—A guide for Westerners. (Rev. ed.). Yarmouth, Maine: Intercultural Press, Inc. A wonderful resource for the Westerner who is just learning about Arab culture. Not only informative in terms of content, but in the range of topics chosen. Highly recommended.

Pipes, D. (Winter 2001). Disappearing Christians in the Middle East. *Middle East Quarterly*, Article 1050, from http://www.danielpipes.org/article/1050 This article brings to light the problem of Christian extinction in the Middle East.

Pipes, D. (Winter 2003). Why does the world hate America? *International Economy*, Article 1000, from http://www.danielpipes.org/article/1000 This article (whose introduction is longer than Pipes' article) corrects the myth of "hating America" into "resenting" it.

Robinson, B.A. (n.d.). Druse, Druse, Mowahidoon. Retrieved November 1, 2003, from http://www.religioustolerance.org/druse.htm This page concisely defines the Druze religion and briefly traces its origins.

Salins, P. D. (1997). Assimilation, American Style. New York: HarperCollins Publishers, Inc. Chapter 3 of this book poses many philosophical premises, such as questioning whether the "melting pot" metaphor can actually be applied to America.

Shaheen, J. (1980). The TV Arab, from http://www.adc.org/index.php?id=283&no_cache=1&sword_list[]=shaheen This article discusses the stereotypes that Westerners have of Arabs, drawing upon Shaheen's book, "The TV Arab."

Swaidan, Z., Marshall, K. P., Smith, J. R. (n.d.). Acculturation Strategies: The Case of the Muslim Minority in the United States, from http://www.sbaer.uca.edu/Research/2001/SMA/01sma100.html This article discusses acculturation strategies employed by Americans who are Moslems.

Thompson, A. (2003, November 6). How did U.S. get copy of Arar's lease? *Toronto Star*, from http://www.thestar.com/NASApp/cs/ContentServer?pagename=thestar/Layout/Article_Type1&call_pageid=971358637177&c=Article&cid=1068073812382 This article wonders about the U.S. and how it obtained Maher Arar's lease.

UCLA Language Materials Project. (n.d.). Levantine Arabic Profile, from http://www.lmp.ucla.edu/profiles/profl02.htm This page goes over the various dialects of Levantine Arabic.

University of Michigan-Dearborn Chaldean American Student Association. (n.d.). Historical background, from http://www.umdcasa.com/index.html This page offers much information regarding the Chaldeans, their history, and their present.

University of North Carolina's *American Diplomacy*. (February 2002). From the Editor—Why They Hate America, from http://www.unc.edu/depts/diplomat/archives_roll/2002_01-3/editor_hate/editor_hate.html This article speculates as to the various reasons the Middle East "hates" America.

U.S._Copts. (n.d.). Welcome, from http://pw1.netcom.com/~us_copts/body_index.html This page cites a number of anti-Copt crimes that occurred in the past 20 years.

U.S. Department of Justice, Civil Rights Division. (n.d.).Federal Protections against National Origin Discrimination, from http://www.usdoj.gov/crt/legalinfo/natorigin.pdf This document sets forth the anti-discrimination law concerning foreigners in America.

Wakins, E. (2000). A lonely minority: The modern story of Egypt's Copts. (Rev. Ed.). Lincoln, Nebraska: iUniverse.com This book is a well-written and informative work that tells the modern story of Egypt's Copts. Highly recommended.

Wikepedia. (n.d.). Coptic Calendar, from http://en2.wikipedia.org/wiki/Coptic_calendar This entry provides information about the Coptic Calendar.

Wikipedia. (n.d.). Semitic Language, from http://en.wikipedia.org/wiki/Semitic_languages This page contains a good deal of information about Semitic languages and the categories surrounding them. Many helpful links. Recommended.

Wikipedia. (n.d.). Zahra Kazemi, from http://en.wikipedia.org/wiki/ Zahra_Kazemi This entry tells about the Iranian-born photojournalist who was slain in her nation of birth.

Winkelman, M. (n.d.). Cultural shock and adaptation, from http:// www.asu.edu/clas/anthropology/bajaethnography/shock.htm This page gives a seemingly comprehensive look at cultural shock and cultural adaptation, including the review of studies and other preceding literature regarding the topic. Recommended.

References

Acho, A. (n.d.). The Chaldean Link. Retrieved November 1, 2003, from http://www.umdcasa.com/index.html

Affluenza: PBS program on the epidemic of overconsumption. (n.d.) Retrieved November 1, 2003, from http://www.pbs.org/kcts/affluenza/

Alexandria 2000. (n.d.). The history of Alexandria, Egypt. Retrieved November 1, 2003 from http://www.alexsite.com/html/assort/roman.html

Althen, G. (1988). American Ways: A Guide for Foreigners in the United States. Yarmouth, Maine: Intercultural Press, Inc.

American Civil Liberties Union. (2003, August 26). ACLU says Justice Dept.'s PATRIOT Act website creates new myths about controversial law. Retrieved October 1, 2003, from http://www.aclu.org/SafeandFree/SafeandFree.cfm?ID=13371&c=206

Anderson, G. T., (2003, September 12). The cost of the good life—Spending on stuff seems a never-ending spiral in America; there's always something new to buy. *CNN Money*. Retrieved October 1, 2003, from http://money.cnn.com/2003/09/11/pf/saving/price_of_wow/index.htm

Arab American Institute. (n.d.). Arab American Demographics. Retrieved October 1, 2003, from http://www.aaiusa.org/demographics.htm

Ashabranner, B. (1991). An Ancient Heritage: The Arab-American Minority. New York: HarperCollins, Inc.

Atour: The State of Assyria. (n.d.). Religious Persecution and Ethnic Genocide of Assyrians in the Middle East. Retrieved November 1, 2003, from http://www.atour.com/holocaust

Berry, J. W., (1980) Acculturation: theory, models and some new findings. Retrieved October 1, 2003, from http://www.rrz.uni-hamburg. de/psych-3/seminar/dahme/John%20W.pdf

Brooks, G., (1995). Nine parts of desire: the hidden world of Islamic women. New York: Anchor Books.

Buchanan, P. (n.d.). Why does Islam hate America? Retrieved October 1, 2003 from http://www.iconservative.com/why_does_islam_hate_America.htm

Bury, C., Gizbert, R. (2003, September 26). The Love-Hate Relationship—The Arab World's Mixed Feelings Over America. Retrieved October 1, 2003   from   http://abcnews.go.com/sections/nightline/DailyNews/ WTC_Arab_us_010926.html

Canadian Coalition Against the Death Penalty. (2000, June 1). News articles. Retrieved November 7, 2003, from http://www.ccadp.org/canadavietnam.htm

Canadian Coalition Against the Death Penalty. (2000, June 4). Nguyen Thi Hiep. Retrieved November 7, 2003, from http://ccadp.org/nguyencanada.htm

Canadian Press. (2003, November 6). Sampson lambastes Canada over torture cases. *Toronto Star*. Retrieved November 7, 2003, from http://www. thestar.com/NASApp/cs/ContentServer?pagename=thestar/Layout/ Article_Type1&call_pageid=971358637177&c=Article&cid=1068117068855

Cannuyer, C. (2001). Coptic Egypt: The Christians of the Nile. New York: Harry N. Abrams, Inc.

Chaldean Federation. (n.d.). The lessons of history and the identity of a people. Retrieved October 1, 2003 from http://www.chaldeanfederation.com/ chaldean-page-01.htm

CIA World Factbook (2003). Retrieved October 1, 2003 from http:// www.odci.gov/cia/publications/factbook/index.html

Coming home. (n.d.). Retrieved October 1, 2003, from http://www.usask.ca/ nursing/International/niger/cominghome.htm

Coptic Orthodox Church Network. (n.d.). The Coptic Calendar of Martyrs. Retrieved November 1, 2003 from http://www.copticchurch.net/easter.html

Copts.com (n.d.). Coptic Demands. Retrieved October 1, 2003 from http://www.copts.net/demands.asp

Copts.com (n.d.). Egypt attempts to close a Coptic church. Retrieved October 1, 2003, from http://www.copts.net/detail.asp?id=451

Copts.net (n.d.). Coptic Demands. Retrieved October 1, 2003, from http://www.copts.net/demands.asp

Dorland's Illustrated Medical Dictionary. (n.d.). The "H" section. Retrieved October 1, 2003, from http://www.mercksource.com/pp/us/cns/cns_hl_dorlands.jspzQzpgzEzzSzppdocszSzuszSzcommonzSzdorlandszSzdorland zSzdmd_h_18zPzhtm

Egyptian Sourcebook for Castle Falkenstein-Alexandria. (n.d.). Alexandria. Retrieved November 1, 2003 from http://cfEgypt.www3.50megs.com/Alexandria/Alexandria.html

Electronic Frontier Foundation. (2001, October 25). U.S.A PATRIOT ACT, as passed by Congress. Retrieved November 1, 2003, from http://www.eff.org/Privacy/Surveillance/Terrorism/hr3162.php

Ethnologue.com (n.d.). ISO 639 Code: ara. Retrieved October 1, 2003, from http://www.ethnologue.com/show_iso639.asp?code=ara

Farah, J. (2003, January 3). Christian Persecution by Arafat. *World Net Daily*, Article 30299. Retrieved November 1, 2003, from http://www.worldnetdaily.com/news/article.asp?ARTICLE_ID=30299

Free Maher Arar. (2003, March 14). The plight of Maher Arar. Retrieved November 7, 2003, from http://www.freemaherarar.com

Hate Crime Statistics. (2001). Retrieved October 1, 2003, from http://www.fbi.gov/ucr/01hate.pdf

International Student & Exchange Services, Dalhousie University. (n.d.). Cultural Adaptation. Retrieved October 1, 2003, from http://www.dal.ca/~studyab/GuideForStudents/StageTwo/stageTwo011.html

Khashan, H. (Winter 2001). Arab Christians as symbol. *The Middle East Forum*, 8, Article 4. Retrieved November 1, 2003, from http://www.meforum.org/article/4

Krawchuk, C. (2003, November 6). In depth: Maher Arar. CBC News. Retrieved November 7, 2003, from http://www.cbc.ca/news/background/arar

Lancaster, J., (1997, March 18). After Violent Attacks, Ancient Coptic Minority Fears It Has Become the Target of Islamic Militants. *Washington Post*, page A 12. Retrieved October 1, 2003, from http://home.netcom.com/~us_copts/copts.html

Lithwick, D., Turner, J. (2003, September 8). A guide to the Patriot Act. *Slate Magazine*. Retrieved October 1, 2003, from http://slate.msn.com/id/2087984/

Middle East Council of Churches. (n.d.). Directory of Member Churches. Retrieved October 1, 2003 from http://www.mecchurches.org/links/directory/memberc.asp

Middle East Media Research Institute. (January 6, 2003). Arab Media Reactions to The U.S.-Middle East Partnership Initiative Part III: It's a Zionist/American Plot. Retrieved October 1, 2003 from http://www.memri.de/uebersetzungen_analysen/themen/usa_und_der_nahe_osten/us_initiative_III_06_01_03.html

Nydell, M. K. (2002). Understanding Arabs—A guide for Westerners. (Rev. ed.). Yarmouth, Maine: Intercultural Press, Inc.

Pipes, D. (Winter 2001). Disappearing Christians in the Middle East. *Middle East Quarterly*, Article 1050. Retrieved November 1, 2003, from http://www.danielpipes.org/article/1050

Pipes, D. (Winter 2003). Why does the world hate America? *International Economy*, Article 1000. Retrieved November 1, 2003, from http://www.danielpipes.org/article/1000

Robinson, B.A. (n.d.). Druse, Druze, Mowahidoon. Retrieved November 1, 2003, from http://www.religioustolerance.org/druse.htm

Rouchdy, A. (1974). Research on Arab Child Bilinguals, Arabic Speaking Communities in American Cities. New York: Center for Migration Studies.

Salins, P. D. (1997). Assimilation, American Style. New York: HarperCollins Publishers, Inc.

Shaheen, J. (1980). The TV Arab. Retrieved October 1, 2003, from http://www.adc.org/index.php?id=283&no_cache=1&sword_list[]=shaheen

Swaidan, Z., Marshall, K. P., Smith, J. R. (n.d.). Acculturation Strategies: The Case of the Muslim Minority in the United States. Retrieved October 1, 2003, from http://www.sbaer.uca.edu/Research/2001/SMA/01sma100.html

Thompson, A. (2003, November 6). How did U.S. get copy of Arar's lease? *Toronto Star*. Retrieved November 7, 2003, from http://www.thestar.com/NASApp/cs/ContentServer?pagename=thestar/Layout/Article_Type1&call_pageid=971358637177&c=Article&cid=1068073812382

UCLA Language Materials Project. (n.d.). Levantine Arabic Profile. Retrieved October 1, 2003, from http://www.lmp.ucla.edu/profiles/profl02.htm

University of Michigan-Dearborn Chaldean American Student Association. (n.d.). Historical background. Retrieved October 1, 2003 from http://www.umdcasa.com/index.html

University of North Carolina's *American Diplomacy*. (February 2002). From the Editor—Why They Hate America. Retrieved October 1, 2003 from http://www.unc.edu/depts/diplomat/archives_roll/2002_01-3/editor_hate/editor_hate.html

U.S._Copts. (n.d.). Welcome. Retrieved October 1, 2003, from http://pw1.netcom.com/~us_copts/body_index.html

U.S. Department of Justice, Civil Rights Division. (n.d.).Federal Protections against National Origin Discrimination. Retrieved October 1, 2003, from http://www.usdoj.gov/crt/legalinfo/natorigin.pdf

Wakin, E. (2000). A lonely minority: The modern story of Egypt's Copts. (Rev. Ed.). Lincoln, Nebraska: iUniverse.com

Wikepedia. (n.d.). Coptic Calendar. Retrieved November 1, 2003 from http://en2.wikipedia.org/wiki/Coptic_calendar

Wikipedia. (n.d.). Semitic Language. Retrieved October 1, 2003, from http://en.wikipedia.org/wiki/Semitic_languages

Wikipedia. (n.d.). Zahra Kazemi. Retrieved November 10, 2003, from http://en.wikipedia.org/wiki/Zahra_Kazemi

Winkelman, M. (n.d.). Cultural shock and adaptation. Retrieved October 1, 2003, from http://www.asu.edu/clas/anthropology/bajaethnography/shock.htm

About the Author

Sally Bishai received her B.S. in psychology from Jacksonville University, her M.A. in communication arts from the University of West Florida, and hopes to have finished her Ph.D. by 2007.

Sally teaches intercultural communication at the University of West Florida, and various speech communication classes at Pensacola Junior College and Oka-loosa-Walton Community College. She is also the Editor-in-Chief of X Culture Magazine (www.xculturemag.com), a webzine which features intercultural and interpersonal issues in communication.

Her interests include shopping, debating, philosophizing, arguing, writing and lecturing; furthermore, she's obsessed with photography, music, light, form, thought, ART, and creating things.

Sally is working on her next book, "What NOT To Do—A Guide for Egyptian Americans," and can be reached at ms3asala@aol.com.

0-595-31731-6

www.ingramcontent.com/pod-product-compliance
Lightning Source LLC
Chambersburg PA
CBHW020918290526
45784CB00002BA/602